Praise for *Firedancer*...

"You deserve to create the work you love and use your deepest gifts. This is not a linear journey. It's an inspired and mystical walk. Kami left behind a demanding corporate career to follow her soul's calling and now she's here to show you how you can do the same. Through exercises, insights and her *Pony Ponderings* inspirational messages, Kami will propel you to take the most important journey of your life."

~Tama Kieves, *USA Today* featured Visionary Career Coach
and Bestselling Author of *This Time I Dance!*
Create the Work You Love and *Inspired & Unstoppable:*
Wildly Succeeding in Your Life's Work!

"Kami and I share the same belief: the Universe has a magical way of leading us to our soul-inspired purpose. *Firedancer* opens your heart to the mysterious ways of our world to awaken your heart's deepest dreams and desires. Through beautiful story and thoughtful guidance, this book will take you on a journey to wake up to who you are and how you're meant to share your gifts with the world."

~Lynne Twist, International Bestselling Author of *The Soul of Money*
and Global Visionary, Activist, and Speaker

"Kami's passion, enthusiasm, and gentle guidance ooze through every page of this delightful and practical book. For any woman who yearns for a life with more soul and sizzle, *Firedancer* may just be the perfect spark for your greatest fire yet."

~Nicole Gruel, Transformational Coach and
Author of *Women of the Wise Earth,*
Dancing with Dragons and *Get Naked, Get Happy*

"Kami Guildner in her inspiring book, *Firedancer*, takes you on a journey of self-discovery. This is by far the most important work you can do in your life and Kami is a wonderful guide. If you feel a deep down desire that there must be more in life, this book is for you."

~Karin Volo, Chief Joy Bringer, International
Bestselling Author of *Engage!* and *1,352 Days*

"Throughout the pages of this beautiful book Kami engages you to feel your heart's calling. This is an inspiring and impactful read for any woman looking to create the meaningful next chapter of her life."

~Rachael Jayne Groover, Bestselling Author of *Powerful and Feminine*

"A must-read for women seeking real meaning in their life. After *Firedancer*, it will become impossible to ignore signposts and callings from the Universe."

~Melissa Hughes, Global Business Coach and Consultant and Bestselling Author of *Sole to Soul: How to Identify Your Soul Purpose and Monetize It*, *It's Not Your Daddy's Store*, and *Full Circle*

"Amazing! Kami rolls out an easy-to-follow, yet thorough, path to getting back on the path of YOU with passionate, inviting simplicity. The practices she sets forth work! She has brilliantly woven together her life experience, seamlessly blended with the importance of the natural world and tried and true words of wisdom. Read it. Reconnect to who you are supposed to be NOW. No shame no blame. Go for it!"

~Ariana Strozzi Mazzucchi, Founder of SkyHorse Equine Guided Coaching™ and Author of *Horse Sense for the Leader Within*

"Kami Guildner's warmth and passion permeate every page of *Firedancer*. If you're a woman hearing a calling for something more, this book will inspire you to transform your life."

~Amanda Trosten-Bloom, Principal, Rocky Mountain Center for Positive Change, Co-Author, *The Power of Appreciative Inquiry*

"*Firedancer* will take you on a journey of your own awakening heart—waking up the 'soul cries' within you to listen and take heed of your soul's purpose and live it full out. A true gem for all women on a spiritual path."

~Tara Mullarkey, Sacred Biz Coach for Female Entrepreneurs

"*Firedancer* ignites all that your soul has been longing for. This is a must-read for every soul-seeking woman. Kami's calling to empower passion and purpose will have women launching next chapters all around the world."

~Kate Maloney - *RiseUP* The Movie & Movement, Founder & Executive Producer

"Powerful and inspiring. *Firedancer* will help every woman who reads these pages embody their essence in purposeful intent."

~ Toti Cadavid, Transformational Branding Expert, Contributing Author, *Pebbles in the Pond (Wave Four)*

Firedancer

May the firedancer in
you shine brightly!
Much love,
Kami

Firedancer

Your Spiral Journey to a Life of Passion and Purpose

Kami Guildner

MERRY DISSONANCE PRESS CASTLE ROCK, CO

Firedancer: Your Spiral Journey to a Life of Passion and Purpose

Published by Merry Dissonance Press, LLC
Castle Rock, CO

FIRST EDITION
2016

Library of Congress Control Number: 2016906901

Guildner, Kami, Author
Firedancer: Your Spiral Journey to a Life of Passion and Purpose
Kami Guildner

ISBN 978-1-939919-36-6
1. SELF-HELP/Personal Growth/Success
2. SELF-HELP/Motivational & Inspirational
3. BODY, MIND & SPIRIT/Inspiration & Personal Growth

Book Design and Cover Design © 2016
Cover Design by Victoria Wolf
Cover Image and Scupture by Robin Wight, FantasyWire Ltd.,
http://www.fantasywire.co.uk/
Book Design by Andrea Costantine
Editing by Donna Mazzitelli, The Word Heartiste
Pony Ponderings Inspiration Cards, written by Kami Guildner, Copyright © Syzygy L L C

Dedication

This book is dedicated to my father, Virgil Guildner.
While he never got to see me in this part of my life
journey as a writer, coach, and speaker, he has been
an always present guiding light during this wondrous
transformation that has unfolded in my world. The
lessons he taught me in life and beyond have shaped
me into the woman I am today. Thank you, Dad.

Contents

Firedancer lives within.
The very essence of you.
Embody her presence and she will set you free.
Dance her into motion and let the spiral of her beauty
energetically flow forth.
An abundant painting of possibilities.
Feel the swirling, flowing motion.
See her colorful strands of love, magic and vitality
intermingle with the wonders of our natural world.
She is you.
As woman.
Full of life.
Living.
Alive.
On fire.

Preface

At 16,000 feet, the crisp, thin air leaves me breathless. Each labored step grasps at my lungs, and I stop to rest. On the top of a bare Tibetan mountain with the cold December winds whipping around me, I sit in quiet solitude. The sun shines warmly upon my face. Bundled in fleece and down, the bitter winds cannot penetrate the peacefulness I feel.

As a young child, I always loved to play in the dirt. Atop this mountain, I find my hands seeking, looking, touching, and experiencing the textures of the earth upon which I sit. My fingers examine each stone, picking and choosing the ones that call to me. The sun continues to warm my body and my mind is clear. Stone by stone, I discover colors and textures and feel in my inner depths the energies brought forth by each gift from the earth that I uncover.

As I sweep away a layer of dirt and rocks, a small spiral

seashell surfaces. Jarring my thoughts from the mountain on which I sit, I ask myself, "How can this be?" A seashell in the wilderness of Tibet. Far from any oceans or seas.

I carefully wrap the delicate shell into a half-used tissue buried deep in the pocket of my jacket. As I carefully place the wrapped shell into my pocket, my thoughts wander. *What occurred in the life of this shell that once hosted a small sea animal in the depth of the sea millions of years ago? Where did its journey begin when this land upon which I sit was in a different form, and how did it come to settle 16,000 feet above sea level?* Pondering the voyage this shell took, I know its journey was long and transformational. And without understanding why, I somehow know that its journey and mine are intertwined in a mysterious, magical way.

My journey to this faraway place high atop a mountain was early in my own transformation. I had traveled from my suited life of executive to experience a land unlike any I had ever known. True, I had traveled for what I thought at the time was love and perhaps adventure, but this trip held a much higher purpose, which would in time be revealed. Although I was already hearing *callings*—inner urgings *hinting* at the invitation to delve into who I was and what I wanted for myself—that *knowing* would come much later.

This adventure was sandwiched between a driven lifestyle of working long days and playing in the world of strategy and communication for a company focused only on growing. I considered that lifestyle "normal," and at the time, I believed this was how my life would *be* and *look* forever and ever. But there in the distant, stark mountains of Tibet, I began to hear a more insistent calling for something more. A deep and newfound, but perhaps ancient, knowing was awakening within—a memory perhaps.

As time passed, the spiraling curves of the seashell I'd found began to connect me to something bigger. Unbeknownst to me when I first discovered this ancient spiral shell, there was an ancient soul inside me waiting to be set free from the toils of her corporate world. This Tibetan seashell, which found a new life in the treasures of my home, would join me in a life-changing transformation. It would one day become my teacher, in an unexpected and mystical way, and I would come to understand that this ancient shell had been placed on my life's path for a reason.

Introduction

In *Firedancer*, I share the story that transformed my life's downward spiral into an upward spiral of learning and growth, an ascension that ultimately led me to connect with and begin to live into my life purpose. Months of discovery opened a door for me to learn many important life lessons. I came to understand that there was a difference between "who I was" and "what I did." I wasn't a title. I wasn't the tasks I completed or the accomplishments I had achieved. I wasn't the number of hours I worked in a day or the number of employees I managed around the world. I was much more than that. I had a soul. I had an inner spirit that was, and is, connected to something much larger than me. I had values and talents that weren't about a title, but were and continue to be about the gifts I bring into the world.

More importantly, my personal journey led me back to the ability to hear my own inner voice. I didn't learn this by continuing down the comfortable, familiar circumstantial doors of opportunity. I had to get out on an edge and do the deep work to recognize and become friends with my own essence and gifts. That work helped me interpret the inner callings of my life. It helped me recognize the signposts as they arrived—the clues that pointed my compass in new directions. I would have missed these signposts if I'd continued to focus exclusively on doing and accomplishing. This deep introspective work helped me tune into flashing inspirations that presented themselves and opened my heart to the people who have graced and continue to grace my pathway.

Today, I don't have to go back to 16,000 feet to hear what my heart wants me to know. I merely need to slow down, pause, and tune in. Then the signposts come. They guide me every day because I make time for them. I understand that I am not here to arrive at a targeted end destination, but rather, I am spiraling through the journey of my life, gathering more experiences and life lessons along the way, which take me to the ever-unfolding next phase of my life.

This is my story—weaving the threads of corporate Kami, single mom, daughter, horsey girl, and nature lover into the fabric that is me. My soul journey has taught me how I can bring the best parts of me to the forefront, braid together my passions around women's empowerment, horses, and nature, and find a purpose that is mine and mine alone. My soul journey led me to leave the corporate world in order to help light the soul journeys of others, and that includes YOU.

Your Journey

This book will help you define the spiraling trajectory of your own story—where it started, where it's been, and most importantly, where it's going. This isn't a book just about dreaming and goal setting. There are many great books out there on the tactical ways to manifest what you want in your life.

You're about to embark upon a deeply personal journey—one where you get the opportunity to shape the path of your future trajectory based on your soul's purpose. This journey invites you to fully awaken your soul-given potential and courageously shine your light onto the world. This *is not* a circumstantial journey. It *is* a methodical deep dive to discover the life you're meant to live. It is a discovery of the most important life experiences you've had in your life, providing a pathway to weave your own threads of meaning together.

Your story will be unique to you and unlike any other person's. You will learn to recognize the signposts in your life that are calling for change—those clues that are there to point you in the direction you're meant to go and guide you through important decisions along the way. Signposts are probably already showing up in your life if you've picked up this book. Your heart knows. She's calling.

To accompany you on your journey, I have created a *Firedancer* workbook. This workbook is meant to be your companion as you traverse this spiral-inspired soul journey back to the Essence of You. You can access and download it from my website at KamiGuildner.com/Firedancer. This workbook can be used to encapsulate all of the work you do in *Firedancer*.

As you move through the opportunities for reflection in the following chapters, you will become intimately connected to who you are in this lifetime—to your essence. Together we'll play in the stories that have ignited your life and set your heart afire. You'll remember what brings meaning to your life and re-connect with your strengths and passions.

At the end of each chapter, you'll also find a special gift from me to you to accompany you on your journey. I have cho-sen a card from my deck of *Pony Ponderings Inspiration Cards*, beautifully illustrated by the talented Diana Lancaster, to help bring positive, thought-provoking guidance to your soul path. Inspired by the heart and wisdom of horses, the messages pro-vide a pathway to your deepest inner knowledge, playfully en-gaging your mind, body, emotions, and spirit.

My own journey was significantly enriched by the gifts of nature and all her gifts of reflective space and awareness that flow through her. The whispers heard from animals and our at-tunement to the rhythm of the earth's vibrations shift our con-scious levels. You will have opportunity to find your own inspir-ing places in nature and learn to hear her voice dance through your body. Nature provides a wide-open vessel to engage your curiosity, to slow down and tune in, and to learn from your in-ner soul messages.

It is from this connected place—the knowing of your in-ner soul that comes from the very deepest part of your ancient wisdom—that you are able to suddenly open the door to your heart's calling. In this quiet place of realization, you'll begin to hear ideas and thoughts that have been lost in the craziness of everyday life. You will begin to put words to those inner call-ings—the longings for deeper meaning gasping from beneath the crazed frenetic life you've been living.

This heart and soul awakening is the body's knowing—an intuitive sense that we were able to connect with and under-stand as young girls—setting you free to live the life you're here to live. This deep knowing guides you to wonderment and a sense of awe. Most importantly, it brings you back to a deep love of life. It unfolds your journey and invites you to intimately know your inner essence. This, therefore, is a journey to your soul—setting your life on fire with passion and daring prowess.

I use the terms essence and soul, which, from my perspec-tive, are two separate yet connected aspects of our Self. Our essence is a culmination of our life experiences, gifts, talents, passions, and values. It is who we are when we show up at our very best. It is what others see when our light shines most bril-liantly—when our personality is at its brightest.

Our soul is deeper and perhaps even more ancient, tran-scending across many lifetimes. Our soul is an inner light that can be set on fire. A friend of mine shared, "The soul knows what we need to learn in this lifetime and takes us on that jour-ney." I believe that when we live fully in the bright light of our essence, the journey of our soul expands and accelerates into purpose and meaning.

The exact path of this journey before you is unknown. In fact, I can promise you that it will not be linear or easy. There will be obstacles, resistance, fears, tears, and perhaps even loss. I will show you how to recognize these quaking moments and step through them with grace. I can assure you that if you persist with a steady truth-seeking intention, you will break through to a life of vibrancy, love, and truth. Ultimately, you will connect with your purpose and discover the song in your heart that's meant to be sung.

1

Corporate Girl

"It doesn't interest me what you do for a living.
I want to know what you ache for and if you dare to dream
of meeting your heart's longing."
~ Oriah Mountain Dreamer

I would become a corporate girl through and through. I was only eighteen when I landed my first corporate job as a receptionist at a downtown oil and gas company. This first taste of corporate life was a stark difference to my farm country childhood in small town America.

I had grown up on a ten-acre farm with horses and dogs and free roam of the Colorado plains. My father's steady blue-collar job provided in a way that never had us wanting for anything. My stay-at-home mom carted my brother, sister, and me to our sports practices and school activities as well as a plethora of horse shows.

Just twenty miles to the south of this farm country upbringing, drawn to the bright lights of the big city, the seeds of corporate Kami were planted. The big city had always intrigued me … tall office buildings, luxurious corner suites, smartly dressed colleagues, visions of grandeur, prestige, and possibilities. I hungered to be a part of this big-city corporate life in a bigger way.

Bored with the mundane tasks of only answering the phone, I asked for more tasks to fill my days. Within just a few short months after starting my receptionist job, I found myself promoted into the engineering department as an engineer tech, learning about spreadsheets and computers and economics. This early taste for learning and achievement, and the rewarding advancement that followed, started the trajectory of my corporate career that would define my existence for the next twenty-five years.

Then, at the young age of twenty, I became a mother. Motherhood was not the path I had planned in these early working years. But this beautiful, happy baby boy would be a blessing that would forever shape my life. At twenty-four, I divorced his father and walked into the role of single mom. The sudden terror that comes with single motherhood, raising questions such as, "How will I put food on the table for my young growing son?" added fuel to my corporate girl dreams.

One evening, on the way home from work, I stopped at the store for dinner and had to scrape the change from the bottom of my purse to pool together enough money to buy groceries for the night. On that fateful day of change-scraping fear, I declared in Scarlett O'Hara style, "I will never again depend on a man to put food on my table to feed my son." I grasped the soils of my life and further fueled my burning drive to succeed. But first, I realized, I would need a college degree.

Night school—bounded by days at the office and wedged between playful moments with my son—shaped my life. My sister often took on night babysitting duties. The every-other-weekends that my son spent with his father provided time for homework, and even the Sunday mornings when my son was home with me were known as Homework Sunday. My rambunctious son grew up learning how to entertain himself quietly on those Homework Sunday mornings, as I wrote papers and studied for exams.

Those early years set a pattern of hard work. My oil and gas company job in the engineering department paid the bills and kept food on the table, even if it was occasionally Kraft Macaroni and Cheese or Top Ramen noodles. My son and I were making it work. In a sense, we were growing up together.

Over the course of growing up together, my life was good. I learned, I grew, I stretched. After I graduated from college, I had the opportunity to take on bigger roles, first moving into the oil and gas software industry as a support rep for the software that I had been using in my engineering tech jobs, and eventually as a marketer. My son moved into young adulthood, and I had more time to dedicate to the growth of corporate me.

With more time for work, I threw myself into the passion of the work and allowed my drive for success to really ignite. I landed the vice president of marketing role, which I had sought for a long time, in a rapidly growing company that would afford me many exciting projects and opportunities for growth. I passionately led multiple complex brand launches and the integration of several major acquisitions, and developed and launched a leadership development initiative for our high potential thought leaders. We had customers in every corner of the world and my own global team spanned five continents across the world. I got to travel and see places that I never thought I'd visit. I loved the diverse cultures in which I worked, the complexity of the problems we solved, and the people I led and collaborated with. It truly was an exciting time in my life.

My life's successes up to this point had been circumstantial. Their very foundations were based on the necessity to put food on the table—to provide for my son. It wasn't as if I had ever sat down and considered, "What am I really great at?" "What parts of my work do I love most?" "Is this truly what I want to be doing?" I merely knew the right people at the right time, and I tailored my life with hard work to open door after door.

Over the course of many years, that hard work opened doors to six-figure salaries, ludicrous bonuses, and executive titles. I was making more money than the farm girl I once was had ever imagined possible. Ambition and drive fueled each advancement and new opportunity. Of course, with every new endeavor, I worked harder, longer hours. Each reward propelled me to repeat the cycle and work even harder the next time around.

On the surface, I had arrived. I envisioned what I wanted, set goals, and consistently check-marked their successful achievement. I was a doer. I was a metric tracker. Someone who could make things happen. My ego lauded my position and loved my vice president title. In fact, in a sense, I had become my title. I knew no other sense of me. Sadly, I couldn't even see I was in this state.

I Lost Me

Somewhere in my corporate climb to the "top," I lost me. Any inherent soul messages wanting to be heard within were hushed by the drive. I let my to-dos define me. My what-I-achieved made up my self-worth.

I pushed aside insecurities and fears by developing a professional persona of who I thought I should be. I let the titles define me. I didn't make time for the things that filled me up. My spirit self was empty.

My life was aligned with the needs and demands of an always hungry corporation—and I bought into the game of letting it drive my life in hungry pursuit of the next promotion. This duo-driven hunger for more spiraled into a crazy cycle. It was in this hunger that I allowed a persona to evolve—a persona that fit the mold of what I thought I should be. A persona that was based in title and prestige. A persona that somehow conveniently forgot other significant pieces of who I was.

What was missing in that persona was significant, even if I didn't recognize it at the time. That little girl growing up on the plains amongst the wheat, the birds, and the horses was completely absent. There was a much softer and deeper side of me within, but she was hidden away. I was squelching my intuitions, my passions, and my values in a soulless existence, as I tried to satisfy the hunger of success and achievement. I was living in motion, without purpose.

Yet, in the midst of this ongoing crazy cycle, my heart was calling. I was getting signs in many forms. I had a sense that something was missing in my life—there was a hollowness I felt within myself. No matter what I did or accomplished, I didn't feel filled up or complete. There was a longing for more. I didn't know what that would, could, or should look like, and most certainly didn't know how to find *it*—whatever *it* was.

That seashell in the ancient Tibetan dust at 16,000 feet brought signs. In the vast open space, in the peace and quiet of the Tibetan mountains, I heard my inner voice that I had stifled for so many years. She called to me saying, "Yes there is more."

The magical, majestic Himalayan mountains started a fire in my soul—a stirring within, a seeking, a restlessness. A spiritual knowingness sought to be awakened. I could feel a newfound curiosity inside my tired body—although I didn't know how to feed this sensation, because it was so far removed from the reality of my normal day-to-day life. As I returned from Tibet and re-entered the stream of this normal way of living, I got my next sign in a dream.

The Dream

I awoke abruptly, conscious of how seemingly real this dream had been. Still invigorated by the experience, I lay there reliving the journey I had just taken. At the start of the dream, I felt tension—a restricted state of mind, my energy blocked. In this dream state, I experienced a dark pool of frustration—feeling stuck and unable to move in a lackluster, colorless, and passionless space.

With beauty and light, my real-life beautiful gray mare, Destiny Dancer—now with wings—suddenly and gracefully flew into the scene, bringing with her trees and mountains, rocks, and the vibrant, vivid colors of the outdoors. We were unexpectedly moved into a peaceful scene of rivers, butterflies, and birds. As Destiny Dancer approached me, I could sense her gentle calm and self-assuredness. There was a knowing way about her, and she seemed to almost smile, which warmed my heart and lifted my mood. As she nuzzled me, her warm breath gave life to my body and a new glow began to shine in, through, and all around me.

With great ease and the gentleness of a mother's touch, Destiny wrapped her legs around me and lifted us into flight with her powerful, giant wings. It was a seemingly natural and effortless launch—so much so that I did not even realize we were in flight until we were well above the land.

As we glided low to the earth, weaving amongst the mountains, trees, and valleys, I felt joy encompass my entire body, ignited by the beauty of all that was around us—the smells of the flowers, the humming of the bees, and the greatness of the eagles with whom we shared the sky. She carried me across the mountains and spiraled out over the open plains—close enough to the earth's surface that I could see the grasses blowing softly in the breeze beneath us.

Destiny was guiding me through nature, and the experience filled my soul. When I awoke, it was with a sense of awe and wonderment—a glow in my heart that I'd felt long, long ago as a child and young adult.

At the time, I didn't quite know the meaning of this dream, but I knew that it was important. I felt its significance. In my twenties and thirties, I often dreamed that I could fly easily and effortlessly—as if it were the most natural thing in the world to do. Flying dreams weren't surprising, since I was on a tremendous path of growth at that time in my life.

Because of my reoccurring flying dreams, especially in my thirties, I'd researched their meaning. Dreams of flying symbolize a sense of freedom and personal growth fueled with passion. Flying dreams can signify a time when everything is flowing smoothly and in control—aligned to one's destiny. They can also provide strength and motivation for us to take responsibility for something in our lives that is spiraling out of control. By the time I was in my late thirties and early forties, my flying dreams had virtually stopped.

I believe Destiny flew into my dreams that night to shed light on the fact that it was time for me to make a correction in my path and realign, even reconnect, with my passions. The power of this great horse lifted me into flight that night to remind me of that sense of wonderment and awe I'd experienced so often in my earlier years.

This dream was also the start of understanding what horses could teach me. The spiritual awakening that had begun on a

Tibetan mountaintop stirred within, beckoning me to go deeper. And I would soon discover that horses would be the ones to show me the way.

I'd known horses from the time my daddy held me atop our horse's back when I was a baby. As a young girl, I had years of working, training, and loving horses. They taught me responsibility, passion, work ethic, and confidence. In fact, I often attributed my corporate girl success to many of those horse-taught skills, which were rooted solidly in my foundation.

At the time of my dream with Destiny Dancer, something had started to shift inside. Something was asking, "Is this really it?" My dream underscored that question, although I didn't understand its meaning at the time. As powerful as my dream was, as much as it impacted me when I awoke, I unconsciously set it aside for another day when I would be more willing to listen to the message that needed to be heard.

Looking back, I eventually realized that this dream came at a time when my job had begun to spiral into a place of battles, frustrations, and my own dislike for the demands of doing more with less. People became less important and the drive for the organization's mighty dollar filled each day. I was regularly tasked with identifying who would be laid off in the next RIF—reduction in force—a term I came to despise. RIF dehumanized the faces and lives of the people impacted by these high-level decisions. With each round of layoffs, I had to reallocate responsibilities amongst my team—demanding that each remaining person take on more and more, requiring them to work harder and dedicate longer hours with fewer rewards. High stakes politics, broken promises, and complex turf battles shifted my previously shining perception of a job I had once loved. And in the midst of the chaos and turmoil, something inside of me began to stir.

Reflection

What is your most memorable dream? Have you had reoccurring dreams in your lifetime, or have your dream patterns shifted, especially more recently? Consider what underlying message might be there for you to interpret? What does your soul want you to know that you might not understand today? You don't have to be a dream interpreter to find meaning in your dreams. Just be curious about your dreams and make time to ponder their significance. Journal about what you observe and see what comes forth.

To the right is your first Pony Ponderings Inspiration Card to start your journey.

Dawn Dreamers

Through the mist of the early morning light secrets are shared. Dawn Dreamers whisper.

There is a message to hear. New possibilities are on the horizon. Close your eyes. Consider the colors you see. Feel the groundedness that Mother Earth provides you. Today is a day begun in peacefulness – let that feeling carry you through your day.

Glimpses of new paths are on the horizon. This is the birthplace of unfolding opportunities – your seeds of life have been planted. You only need to nurture these budding dreams. Take time to live in these possibilities today. Acknowledge them. Write them down. Paint the pictures and envision where these dreams will take you. Dreams are your gift.

2

The Universe's Plans

"There is one great truth on this planet: whoever you are,
or whatever it is that you do, when you really want something,
it's because that desire originated in the soul of the universe."
~ Paulo Coelho, *The Alchemist*

Just a few months after the dream and in the midst of all the chaos in my work environment, a series of life-changing circumstances occurred. My role as corporate Kami had served me well, but apparently there was something more for me to do in this world. It was time for me to move forward in my journey and discover my true purpose in this life. Since I wasn't about to willingly leave the comforts of the persona I had built, the Universe took over.

On that fateful day, I sat across from my boss of only six

months. "I have some bad news," he said. "I'm really sorry to inform you that your job has been eliminated … and there's not a single other role anywhere in the company for you."

I was stunned. I was being laid off! *How can they let me go?* For the past seven years I'd been a rising star in the company—working eighty-hour weeks on the tough projects that no one else wanted! I could feel the anger rise within me. *How dare he!* I could feel the tears welling up inside, too, but I kept telling myself that I mustn't let him see me cry.

More thoughts ran through my head. *What about my team? Who will lead them? Who will protect them? What will they think? And what will others think?* After all, I'd lived a "favored status" for most of my career, rising easily from promotion to promotion. With the simple swipe of his pen, he was taking all of this away.

Within the hour, I left the building for the last time, with seven years of this company in one small box. I left that day with no computer and no Blackberry, which were the lifelines to my days and nights. Most importantly in my mind, I left on that fateful day stripped of my identity as a vice president of marketing.

The First Morning

The next morning, I arose at 5 AM, because that's what I did every day. This day, however, I had no overseas calls to make, no emails to answer. In fact, I didn't even have the technology that made any of this possible. The first task of the day was to be at Costco when the doors opened, so that I could equip myself with technology—a new computer and a new Blackberry. I needed to begin my search for my new job, my new life ... my new identity.

I rushed home to log on and decided to look at my email first. There was an overwhelming outpouring of support and kindness from my coworkers all around the world. Many of them shared my anger and my sadness. And many of them told me, "Take some time ... slow down ..."

Yeah, yeah, I said to myself. I was focused on finding the next job. *Who should I reach out to? What companies should I target? Which ones look most attractive?* I got more emails telling me to "Take some time ... slow down ..."

I realized I was starting to see a theme. *Maybe they're right,* I thought. *Maybe I do need a break.* So I made a deal with myself. I decided that I'd give myself a month—a month to play, a month to reconnect with friends I'd lost touch with, a month to ride my horses, a month to get out in nature. One month—that was it! Afterwards, I'd start my job hunt ... on August 1, 2008.

The Universe Has Different Plans

Once more, the Universe had different plans. As the month was winding down—on July 29, 2008 to be exact—I got a phone call. My father had died.

My world stopped. Nothing else mattered. In my sadness, I started pondering the lessons I had learned from my father.

He taught me about the importance of family and of loving his spouse—my mother—from his deepest core. He taught me to be true to my friends. He taught me to ride a horse. He taught me the responsibilities of caring for animals. He taught me about the love of nature. And he taught me that it was easiest to talk to God in nature.

With all these thoughts, I wrote a poem about all the life lessons he had taught me. In writing it, I started to see glimpses of me—glimpses of the "me" that I'd somehow lost along the way. These were my first clues that it was time to *take time* to focus on me, that it was time to find myself again.

In those early days of sorrow, I discovered that the best place to find myself was in nature. Each morning, as I cleaned the barn, I took the time to just sit and watch moments of nature, like baby swallows as they took their first flight. I pondered the wonders of our world. I watched in awe as a hawk flew up out of a ditch with a snake in its beak, and I contemplated the cycles of life. On many days, I cried into my horse's mane and felt her strength lift my heart back towards happiness.

I took time to recall memories of my father with my mother, my sister, my brother, and me. I shared childhood stories with my son and smiled at the good fortune that he'd had the opportunity to know his grandfather into his young adult years.

For many months, I continued my journey of rediscovery, taking meaningful time with friends, journaling, hiking, and simply sitting. Just being. Ultimately, I began to remember me.

Reflection

Have there been times in your life when the Universe has delivered an unexpected course correction to you? Jot them down. Consider if there were important shifts in your life that occurred after that course correction—perhaps shifts that might not have occurred if your life course hadn't been altered.

Wisdom of Your Ancestors

In the dark of a crescent moon, a horse moves steadily through the night. Over rocks and trails and mountaintops – despite the darkness – finding light in his inner instincts to take him to his morning destination. It's a wisdom ingrained from his ancestors who walked before him.

Ancient paths of those who walked before you can lead you through any darkness. Tap into the wisdom of your ancestors and allow your soul to radiate the way.

Consider what messages they might bring to you. Connect to your inner wisdom and you will know which path to take – for daylight always follows darkness.

3

Signposts, Callings and Gifts from the Universe

"When you want something, all the universe
conspires in helping you to achieve it."
~ Paulo Coelho

During those last years of my corporate life, I got plenty of signposts that the Universe had different plans for me. My body was saying "No!" to the crazy-busy pace of my life with a constant onslaught of colds and flus. I was tired, worn out, and exhausted. I had a deep sense of dread when I arrived at the office each morning as I anticipated what the day had in store for me.

I wanted a meaningful long-term relationship in my life—a spouse—but I really didn't have time to date. And speaking of relationships, my work relationships were a mess. I was at odds with my longtime favorite boss of all time after having a major blowout disagreement. And then one of my employees, who had worked for me at three different companies over the course of fifteen years, looked at me one day and said, "I don't even know who you are." I dismissed her comment with the thought, *She just doesn't understand my busy executive life.*

Yes, I was seeing all kinds of signposts, but I wasn't paying attention. The challenge was that I didn't know another paradigm for my life even existed. I knew no alternate routes. Working in the corporate world was all I had ever known. After all, I had to earn a living. I had a mortgage to pay. I had horses to feed. I was hearing a calling for more, but I felt stuck and wedged into a life that seemed to have no other paths. I didn't know what to do, and I certainly didn't know *what* was calling to me. For the first time in my life, I didn't know where my life was going.

For the majority of us, we've been given roadmaps our whole lives. We journey from kindergarten to elementary school, from middle school to high school, and onto college. Then we land that first job, combine it with hard work, and move into our first promotion. We meet the person of our dreams and move on to create a family, then acquire a house, a car, and a mortgage. We continue to work until retirement. Ultimately, along come grandkids to complete the cycle of living according to what society deems a "good life." Life is full of norms, both spoken and unspoken, for what *should* be next in our life.

The courageous souls who dare to step outside the predefined yellow brick road of yesteryear, by listening to the sign-posts that show up in their lives and seeking to answer the call-ings that are whispered in the winds of their lives, will discover a more meaningful journey. Yet, most of us get caught in the day-to-day rhythm of numbing monotony and live busy lives where we struggle to balance crazy long hours at work with the demands and *expectations* of raising a family, rarely turning off the noise of life. The outer noise is always on, with little to no time for self-care or self-awareness.

When we stay in this noise too long, we begin to make state-ments like:

- ▲ "I feel stuck and exasperated."
- ▲ "I'm bored and don't really care."
- ▲ "I'm hearing a calling for something more, but I don't know what it is."
- ▲ "I feel lost."

It can be confusing when you think there might be some-thing else you are supposed to be doing in your life, yet there is no roadmap to take you there. Chances are, however, if you're feeling or expressing any of the above statements, you have al-ready been experiencing signposts. Signposts are offerings of ways out of the confusion.

Signposts

Signposts show up in in our lives in all sorts of ways. They come in our dreams, like my own dream when my gray mare Destiny

Dancer took me flying, abruptly awakening me and leaving me breathlessly pondering a deeper meaning to my life. They come in small messages that only our inner knowing can hear—if we allow ourselves to listen. The messages can show up in our lives in conversations and in the synchronicity of events. Signposts are in the stories we tell over and over again.

Sometimes signposts come in numbers or a specific word that just keeps repeatedly showing up. A friend of mine, Karen, shared the following with me in writing:

"I started seeing "11 11" randomly a few years ago, but when I realized it was happening more and more frequently, I started to pay attention. First, it was the clock. I would randomly glance at a clock at the exact moment of 11:11. What really made me chuckle was that sometimes I wouldn't even look at a clock any other time of the day or night!

"Now I see 111s and 11 11s in addresses, receipt totals, car license plates, or my odometer when I glance down at that exact moment it turns to mile 111. I've been given 11 as my number for waiting in line, or I glance at a thermometer and it's 11 degrees. Even as I write this, I'm working on a paper that someone sent over for me to edit, and at the bottom it says, 'Revision 11/11!' And the email you sent asking me about this phenomenon came at 11:11. Cracks me up!!"

When I asked her what she thought the rise of 11 11 in her life meant, she quickly replied, "New beginnings. Moving forward into the unknown. New places, new people, new purpose." All the changing circumstances of her life since the numbers started to occur reflect just this.

Karen's interpretation of this meaning is hers and hers alone.

While others may seek to offer their perspective to the meaning of a signpost, ultimately, what each of us interprets and understands for ourselves in our own journey is really what counts. In her soul messages, Karen found clarity that she could trust. As she lives into the life transformations she encounters, more transformation comes and the spiral of her journey accelerates. This is the beauty of discovering the signposts in our lives.

Signposts can come to us from nature, such as from the birds and other wildlife. For instance, have you ever had a specific animal in nature show up in your life over and over again? Perhaps it is a robin or sparrow that keeps visiting on your windowsill. The next time this occurs, allow yourself to tune into your visitor with awareness. As you do so, you'll most likely find that you want to stop and be completely in the moment—just you and that bird enjoying a few seconds of connection. Tune into your curiosity. What were you thinking when the bird showed up? Be curious about where that bird has been and why it is there with you in that moment. Simply ask, "Is there a message for me today?" and see what transpires from your inner voice. Let your imagination play!

Animal Speak author Ted Andrews calls this our creative imagination. He wrote, "Most people equate the imagination with unreality. Nothing could be further from the truth. The imagination is a power of the mind to create and work with images. It is this ability which can open us to other realms, assist us in healing, help us discover lost knowledge and open to higher vision."

There is a huge inner awakening that occurs when we start to tune into the details in our life at this level. You create space for thought and ideas. Yes, sometimes that bird might just be there for no reason at all; however, it also might be the key that unlocks a locked imagination that is keeping you stuck. It's worth a curious pondering.

Signposts can also come to you as you walk through the woods in a quiet snowshoeing experience or on a contemplative beach run. You are merely giving yourself space for your monkey-mind to shut down and then hear an inner wisdom. Signposts are our intuition asking for our inner wisdom to be set free.

We can choose to explore these signposts as they come to us and explore the deeper calling that is whispering to us, or we can ignore them, like I did in my last corporate working years. The catch here is that the Universe will eventually deliver a catalyst shift of some sort if we ignore these signposts—a shift that will forever change the trajectory of our lives.

I recently had the opportunity to see tech leader Tom Chi speak at the inaugural Success Summit 3.0 Conference. Chi led the technology teams of Google Glass and Google's Self-Driving Car and worked on innovative projects, developing the likes of Microsoft Outlook, Yahoo Search, and Yahoo Answers. He was at the peak of this amazing career when he got a course correction. His lower GI tract ruptured, and almost instantly, he lost forty percent of his blood supply. As he was rushed into the emergency room, he had to be given four simultaneous blood transfusions to save his life, and four more during the night. When he awoke the next morning, the nurse said to him, "I'm glad you're here, you were a minute away from your brain dying."

Thus began his course correction. He left Google and began to travel the world. He started to experience some of the third world challenges firsthand, and the engineer/scientist/designer in him began to see solutions. He saw the challenges around unsanitary water, and his inventive mind began to build ways he could solve those problems. He said to himself, "Solving the most important problems in the world deserves the best tools."

Today, Chi commits his brilliant mind power to solving our most important global problems. There's no doubt in my mind that Chi's gifts are better served in the work he's committed to today. As painful and dangerous as his course correction was, the Universe had bigger plans for his talents. Our world needs his gifts, and his pathway was significantly shifted to enable him to step into this newfound purpose, which will no doubt make an impact on our world forever.

The foundational shifts that occur when we don't heed these messages can come in many different ways. I hear stories every day about someone significantly changing their life path after the Universe delivered a course-correcting catalyst. It might be a health scare like Chi's, a job loss like I experienced, a parent or close friend's death—something that shakes our very center and takes us off balance from the path we've been on.

When you start to recognize the signposts in your life, you awaken to a deeper understanding that life is short and there is meaning to why you are here. This awakening changes you inside. Your heart radiates a deeper yearning. Your courage expands exponentially. You begin to trust in the lessons that come your way. And in the rare moment you find time for quiet personal reflection, wild and uplifting ideas are birthed. Ideas that pose the question, "What if ...?" This is how you start to hear your calling.

Callings

You may be saying, "I don't know what my calling is. I just know there's something more." The first thing I want to say to you in response is, "This is normal!" Our society isn't wired to think about our purpose in life from a young age. Like my own journey, chances are your journey has been circumstantial and a result of mixing hard work with the various opportunities that presented themselves.

My intention is to take you on a new type of journey that starts to open up possibilities you haven't thought about before. This journey will help you reconnect to yourself at your very essence and invite you to begin to ask the questions that will provide clues to your calling. It will help you think outside the box of what you do today to what is possible beyond. Finally, it will offer you the opportunity to become aware of what it feels like to get a calling.

Before we go any further, let's define a calling. Callings are a deep longing to bring more of something into your life. Callings represent a longing that won't leave us and puts us into a state of continuous seeking for something beyond where we are at present.

Author Gregg Levoy, in his book *Callings*, wrote, "—Our callings—... [can be] in the areas of work, relationship, lifestyle or service. They may be calls to *do* something (become self-employed, go back to school, leave or start a relationship, move to the country, change careers, have a child), or calls to *be* something (more creative, less judgmental, more loving, less fearful). They may be calls toward something or away from something; calls to change something …; calls toward whatever we've dared and double-dared ourselves to do for as long as we can remember."

The interesting thing for me personally was that I read Levoy's book about ten years before I left the corporate world. It spoke to me, but I didn't know why at the time I read it. I didn't understand that I was already being called and that I had a great journey in front of me. However, in reading that book, more of the seeds of what lay ahead were planted.

Your calling may be to take on a bigger presence in a role or field you're already in today. Your calling may be to put a different lens on the skills and talents you've built over your entire life and apply them in a whole new way. Your callings may be big leaps in completely new directions or small steps toward a refinement of the life you are already living.

For example, in the past year, I have had a calling for more ocean time. I love my home in Colorado, but we are landlocked. Sometimes, I just have the desire to hear the waves and infuse my soul with the energy of the sea. I have listened to this calling, and we've been to the Oregon Coast twice this year. When we were there, I danced wildly with the wind on the beach and did comical fifty-year-old cartwheels. I hadn't done cartwheels in years, and even when I did do them more frequently, I wasn't very good at them. Being at the beach, it didn't matter how they looked. While we were at the coast, I felt vibrantly alive and passionately aware of the beauty and power of our world. I felt it in every part of my body from head to toe.

Yet, I began to wonder if the call to the ocean was bigger than I thought, whether it actually represented more than taking some time at the beach. In this state of free-spirit play, my creativity came alive. I started writing and working on material that had sat stagnant for nearly a year. The energy of the ocean unlocked my writer's block and gave me a new boost of momentum. I truly believe there is a connection, not only to listening to the calling to travel to the ocean, but in every calling I heed. Each calling is a part of my interconnected journey.

Deciding to head to the Oregon Coast was an easy calling to follow. Callings like these are meant to simply feed our souls and our bodies. Our bodies know what we need, if we listen. They are tied to our internal natural rhythms.

Other callings are much more grandiose. They are life-giving. They are powerful guiding lights that take us in directions we may not even understand. Sometimes these callings are even tied to our life purpose. Answering a calling with large life transformational choices is not easy. You may feel resistance. You may not trust your inner voice, or you might make up excuses. You may hear yourself saying things like, "Life is too crazy busy and the time isn't really right."

Here's what I know about these powerful callings and the accompanying excuse that "the time's not right":

1. These callings are a gift. When they come, they are yours and yours alone, which allows you to feel them intimately. Whether you believe it or not, your journey

has prepared you for them when they come. You have the tools and resources to listen and evolve your journey into what's next. Trust that the Universe has provided you the right experiences and knowledge to grow into this calling. It will most likely feel like a stretch and it will probably feel uncomfortable. If you're willing to listen deeply, it is a calling to step into a bigger platform of your life and play bigger.

2. Your self-critic will show up in a big way when you get a calling for something more. She will tell you you're not smart enough, clever enough, or strategic enough. She will throw you into a swirl of scarcity-thinking: not enough resources and not enough time. Know this: your self-critic is always wrong!

3. Fear feeds your claim that "the time's not right." You may push fear aside and ignore it. You may even say it's not there. But it won't work. Fear doesn't just go away or lay dormant. It will fester inside and burst forth at the most inopportune times. When you step into your fear and become intimately connected to it, you can transform the energy of fear to an energy of courage—a fire that can't stop you.

4. When we don't heed our calling, the Universe will eventually take over with a course correction. Health issues, job problems, family crises, and other major catalytic shifts make their way into our lives until they force us towards new decisions. It is more efficient and less painful to move into action on our callings when they knock at our door while we have a solid

foundation beneath our feet, and before a major course correction presents itself.

Several years ago, my own coach said to me, "Your gift is meant to matter, and today … right now … there are people who need your gift. Who are you to withhold this gift from the world?" That hit me hard. It gave me new courage. And so I now say to you, "Your gift is meant to matter, and today … right now … there are people who need your gift. Who are you to withhold this gift from the world?"

Your journey through this book will help you recognize the signposts, decipher your callings, and walk through the emotional obstacles that attempt to waylay your path. Finding your calling will transform your life. Take it from someone who has found hers. When you step into your own calling, you will live a passionate, meaningful life full of vitality and purpose. There is no greater gift to you and to those in your life. You will be a shining example of living life to its fullest. Is that not the model of life you'd like to portray?

Gifts from the Universe

There is something absolutely amazing about discovering your calling—the moment you know it, all things in your life start to shift to make way for it. It's like the Universe knows that you are ready. For instance, a new person shows up in your life who has knowledge about something you need to learn. Or you run across an article or class that is perfect for you. Maybe someone tells you they need your help in a way that is related to your calling. Effortlessly and instantaneously, gifts start to drop into your lap.

Sometimes the Universe delivers gifts that will prepare us for the journey ahead, even when we don't understand the reason at the time. For example, I met my husband, Tim, the day after Thanksgiving 2007, on a match.com date, just seven months before I would lose my job and eight months before I would lose my father. At a rustic mountain town bar, I met my life soul partner—the man who would become my rock in the moments of despair that would transpire over the next year. I don't believe it was a coincidence that I met Tim just a few months before my world fell apart at the seams. I think the Universe knew I was going to need love and support around me in order to move forward in my life.

The interesting thing was that I had been serially single most of my adult life. It wasn't as if I hadn't wanted a long-term relationship for all those years. I had met many and tried on lots for size, with none of them sticking. What I know now is that being single allowed me to really grow as an individual. For that, I am thankful. I'm even more thankful that Tim swept me off my feet when he did.

On the day I lost my job, he looked me in the eye and said, "Don't worry, you'll find something better and we'll make this work together." He believed in me. Tim held me tight the day I lost my father and kept me on my feet. At my father's memorial he was my strength, and I remember leaning into his strong arms that day.

One year later, when we planned to spread my father's

ashes sixteen miles deep into the wilderness of the San Juan Mountains in southwestern Colorado, my son and my non-horsey Tim backpacked the first eight miles, while fourteen of us rode horses up the rough terrain to my father's hunting camp. I remember waking in our tent on the morning we would continue our ride an additional eight miles up to 12,000 feet elevation, up the canyon that was known amongst his hunting buddies as Virg's Canyon … my dad's canyon. We were going to spread his ashes that day at his favorite rock, deep in the San Juan wilderness.

Overwhelmed with emotion about the day, I wasn't sure if I wanted to ride or hike this extremely rough terrain. Tim held me that morning and said, "I will do it with you … whichever you want … to ride or hike." And so we rode those sixteen miles that day—eight up and eight back—with Tim alongside me on one of the seasoned pack horses that took care of him while he took care of me. The trails in the San Juans are steep, rocky, and often narrow, with hundred-foot-cliff drop-offs in some places. Even being a seasoned horse person, they shook my nerves. Tim rode like an old cowboy who'd ridden the trails for years. He was there and fully present for me to lean into.

As we rode down the valley, back to the hunting camp that summer evening, out of the midst of the gnarly trails we'd just descended, an eagle followed us overhead through the entire valley. He finally tipped his wings to soar off over the hillside. As I rode beside my brave, strong future husband, I knew our relationship was forever.

In the months that followed, it eventually would be Tim who gave me that extra edge of courage to start my own business—

to step into what I knew in my heart was my calling. Yes, there was no accident that he came into my life when he did. The Universe delivers gifts just when we need them.

Reflection

1. Are there any signposts showing up in your life today? Have you had recurring or memorable dreams recently? Or have any interesting, new people come into your life? Perhaps you just can't get one wild idea out of your head. Record everything that comes to mind. Nothing is insignificant.

2. Begin to be aware of your surroundings and the synchronicities that show up in your life. Do you see a recurring number everywhere you go, or maybe a specific animal keeps showing up on your walk or while driving? Be curious. Consider if this represents anything to you, or research the meaning. Is there a deeper meaning to ponder?

3. We all have an inner critic who speaks to us when we're stepping into something new and larger in our world. Write a list of all the famous inner critic messages you know by heart—you know the ones—that you have told yourself over and over again. Then release them! Burn them! Set them free!

4. Reflect on why this book spoke to you. Write about your reasons for picking it up. After having read up to

this point, record any words that have caught your attention and why they may be significant. What are you seeking in your life that isn't in it right now?

5. Are you hearing callings? Do you know what is calling to you, or do you simply know there's something more for you, even if you cannot yet define or identify it? Go on a walk and ponder these questions. Then, record any thoughts, insights, or even questions that bubbled to the surface.

6. Recall a time in your life when you received a gift from the Universe. It could be a right person who came into your life at the right time, it could be resources that showed up just in time, or it could be as "simple" as having been in the right place at the right time for a certain opportunity to unfold. Tell that story to a friend and ask them if they've ever had a similar situation happen to them.

The Rhythm of Synchronicity

Lines of synchronicity enter our worlds each day. People walk into our lives with new ideas, in new relationship, in perfect timing. Nature swirls motion around us with birds in flight, wildlife passing through, flowers blooming and weather always in change. Is there a message to hear?

Take time today to consider the possibilities. Open your heart to the synchronicity of life. Are the sequence of happenings reflecting your deepest emotions? Or are there new ideas to explore?

Participate in life in active awareness – fully in tune to the rhythm around you. Follow where you are drawn – letting your intuition be your guide. For synchronicity is at play today and you only need listen.

4

Coming Home to You
Through Nature's Gifts

"One touch of nature makes the whole world kin."
~ John Muir

The arc of my journey back to me was grounded in the beauty of nature. Nearly every unfolding lesson or epiphany had a link to the gifts of our earth. Like so many, in my late years of my corporate life, I wasn't getting enough outdoor time. And when I did find myself back in nature, I got powerful insights into my journey. I could see things more clearly and the dots started to connect.

Why does nature provide such a platform for transformation? For me, its expansiveness is a clean slate for possibilities.

I breathe more deeply. Nature's beauty inspires and uplifts my soul. I feel a tactile pull to touch the soils, drawn to the energy forces that radiate around me. In nature, my mind is set free from the toils of worry, fear, and the unknown. My heart is alive with vitality.

The human race historically has spent a great deal of time outdoors in nature. Our ancient ancestors hunted, cooked, and survived in the outdoors. Their spirit world was celebrated and ritualized in the outdoors. The teachings that were passed between generations were told in the outdoors and rooted amongst the animals and cycles of Mother Earth. The last hundred years have increasingly brought people indoors and out of touch with nature.

Our nature-deprived society now lives in a sterile, white-office-walled world with little connection to the gifts that Mother Nature provides. With a cell phone on one ear and a computer at our fingertips, the electronic vibrations of our life drive almost every waking moment. It's no wonder we don't hear the messages from our very selves, because we are bombarded with interruptions nearly every second of our lives.

Our city-dwelling lifestyles of today are filled with long working days in buildings filled with recycled air, florescent lighting, electronic waves, and closed-in spaces. We learn *inside*, we explore our spiritual growth *inside*, and even a large part of our play, as media-driven entertainment has evolved, is *inside* as opposed to taking place outside in nature.

You can even find the definition of "nature deficiency" on *Wikipedia*. Nature deficiency was coined by Richard Louv in his book *The Nature Principle*. In his research, Louv claims that as a whole, people are spending less time outdoors. He has a deep concern about the impact this will have on our children. He faults sensationalist media and paranoid parents for literally "scaring children straight out of the woods and fields," as we keep our children close, giving them little room to explore nature freely. As a result, children have turned to the lure of media and electronic games, drowning their days, overloading their minds, and eventually burying their creative souls.

The Nature Conservancy and *Women's Health Magazine* did a study on how much time women spend in the outdoors. The research showed that while a vast majority (ninety percent) of the women knew that being outdoors was good for their health, only twenty-five percent went outside to try and relieve stress. Worse yet, only forty percent of the women surveyed spent time outside at least one to two days per week. Ten percent didn't get outside at all in any given week.

There is something about the rhythm of nature that shifts us out of these invasive vibrations that fill our lives today. I find the best way to turn off the noise of the electronically-connected life is to come home to me—in the world of Mother Nature's gifts. For me, home is in the animals and the earth beneath my feet. Home is in the nature and mountains where I live. I feel it in my veins, pulsating through my body and inviting new awakenings.

As a little girl I knew this. We lived on the plains of Colorado. Behind my family's ten-acre farm was an open field, bordered only by farmer's corn fields, our distant neighbors, and a railroad track, with farmer's fields beyond that. These expansive eighty acres beyond our farm provided a playground of

discovery for my young heart to explore. The rolling land offered seclusion from all eyes, with a small cattail-lined pond at
its center.

It was here that I felt my first deep connection to earth.
Drawn to the shorelines of the pond, I embraced the soil—cer-
emoniously creating meals of mud, weaving feathers of adorn-
ment into my long hair, imagining myself as the Native American that freely roamed these lands. The birds joined the melody
of my own songs. My beloved horse grazed nearby. He was
a retired racehorse, a strikingly beautiful sorrel Thoroughbred
with four white socks. He was my best friend. And when the
moment struck me, I would swing my lanky young girl legs over
his fifteen-and-a-half-hand back, hooking my ankle on his with-
er, and with strength and ease, pull myself upright to launch
into a gallop across the expansiveness of the land. Together we
were free and fearless.

It was in my childhood experiences that I discovered the
grounding energy of home. Home in nature. Even in the realm
of my life today—no longer corporate jungles but entrepreneurial work from the comfort of my own home—I sometimes find I
spend too much time in front of a computer and disconnected
from nature. Then, I get a call—knocking on the internal door
of knowing within my body. It starts in my neck and shoulders. A tightness begins, emanating from the tension of a busy
mind that hasn't stopped. Tension pulses through my veins. In
response, my body reminds me, "You need to be outside." And
I go. Immediately, nature's gifts wash over my soul and release
the energies that pulsate in chaotic patterns. Once again, I'm
home.

I'm fortunate to live in the foothills above Denver, Colorado, and so am able to wake each day to wooded hillsides filled with wildlife and birds. It's not unusual for me to stop in the middle of my day to enjoy a passing herd of deer. Even after living in this environment for over twenty-five years, I still run to get my camera or simply stop in awe of their beauty. It's a reset button that lights up my heart. My creative capacity increases when I take moments like this.

One of my most proud and creative corporate-world projects was actually conceptualized on my deck on a sunny, warm spring day while I was being serenaded by birds. For months, I had been struggling with the concepts of a program I wanted to launch but wasn't quite connecting the dots. The open space provided a nature-inspired whiteboard that day as I found clarity, which resulted in a global thought leadership program that would become a brand foundation for my company. Eventually, hundreds of people went through this leadership development program and changed the shape of my company's brand around the world. It all started with the seeds that were planted that spring day on my warm sunny deck.

Today, I take my work outside whenever I can. Not only do I often do my own planning and writing outside, I bring clients there to process their journeys. Nature provides a backdrop for us to tune in and hear our own inspiration. To slow down and disconnect. And when we go to this space, things start to shift and move within us.

Reflection

We are going to continue your journey by bringing more nature into your life. It's essential for you to connect with nature in some way. If you miss this important step, you may not hear many of the messages your heart sends to you. Without taking such a pause, the noise of everyday life will continue to be in the way.

I invite you to find home in the grounding that Mother Nature gifts us. By starting here, you will open your heart and body to the journey before you. You will become more aware of the energetic pulsations around you, and you will find wisdom in this peaceful reflection.

Nature is where you can begin to hear your callings again. There's an ancient wisdom in this ground beneath your feet that speaks to the soul, and from this newly reawakened place in your life, you will begin to experience the gentle nudge asking you to listen. Nature will gently awaken your body and ask you if you're here.

Immerse yourself in any one of the experiences in nature that follow, without having to evaluate or understand why you've chosen it. You can do one of these or all of these. Dog-ear this page, and come back to these reflections often as you progress through your own soul journey, as there will be more to learn from nature as you spiral forward.

Body Scan Walk in Nature

Take a moment to scan your body. Start at the very tips of your toes and move up your body, body-part by body-part. Notice where you feel tension. Are there areas of your body that feel differently? Are there areas that feel heavy or light? Warm or cool? Just notice.

Next, take a peaceful, quiet walk through nature. Fully take it in. Enjoy the beauty, the sounds, and the smells. Stop when you notice something that catches your attention and examine it further—whether it's a flower or a bird in a tree overhead. Whatever it is that catches your attention, really see it—its colors, its texture. Imagine how it feels to the touch. Consider if it's warm or cold, soft or hard, and whether there is a smell associated with it. Let your curiosity play.

As you return home, do another scan of your body. What has shifted? What is different about the way your body feels? Just notice and enjoy. You've begun the opening of you.

Schedule Time in Nature

How much time do you spend outdoors? If you are only getting one to two days outdoors, like so many other women, I invite you to look for ways to significantly increase this. Whether it's watching the sunrise while taking your dog on a walk, putting your hands in the dirt as you plant seeds in a garden, breathing in the breath of a horse in silence and introspection (one of my personal favorites), laying in a grove of aspen and watching the sun shine and sparkle against the leaves, dipping your toes into the ocean as you walk barefoot on your beach walk, or any other outdoor activity, get out and do it. This is your journey home. You get to choose the way. In doing so, your creativity, energy, and vitality will blossom.

Nature Shrine

There are some days when we just can't make it out into nature. Perhaps you live in a busy cement-lined city with few outdoor spaces. Perhaps you're attending a conference at a hotel that keeps you busy from dawn to dusk and late into the evening. Perhaps the weather has kept you indoors. No matter the reason, I invite you to create a nature shrine in your home, and even set aside a few items from nature that you can pack and take along on those nature-deprived trips and activities.

Start your collection with items from your favorite place in nature—it might be a rock, a branch, or a seashell. Then begin an intentional, contemplative search for more special gifts from the earth to add to your nature shrine. Look for items that call to you—objects that draw your attention. It might be the shape, color, or the texture that speaks to you. Or perhaps it's special simply because it reminds you of the special location where you found it.

Consider nature's elements: earth, water, fire, and air. Are you drawn to any of these elements? Can you bring those elements into your shrine in some way—perhaps a water fountain, a candle, a prayer flag blowing in the wind out your window, or a special rock?

Is there a special animal that speaks to your heart? You can incorporate a picture or even something from that animal, such as a bird's feather. For example, I have a piece of braided horse mane on my own nature altar.

As you bring together your own private collection of nature, display it in a special place in your home. On your inside-bound days, simply take a few moments during your day to observe, breathe in, hold, touch, and feel the inspiration of nature from your personal nature shrine. See what you notice. Journal about it. Feel your gratitude for these reminders of nature's ongoing support.

Nature-Inspired Creative Burst Day

Set aside a day, or an afternoon, to dedicate to your biggest current creative challenge. Spend the time outside—in a park, on your deck, or even on the beach or a lakeshore. Bring along all you might need to fuel your creativity: flip charts, computer, journal, color markers, post-it notes. Then play in and with the concepts you're considering. Just getting out of your normal environment will shift your creative juices and put them in motion!

Technology Sabbatical

Take a day to turn off all the technology around you. No phones, no computer, no television. Notice your reactions. Do you long to pick up your phone and peek at your email? Do you feel lost for something to do? What do you do with your time instead? How does your body feel being technology free? Journal about your experience and consider what you can learn from a technology sabbatical.

Dance with Mother Earth

The following is a "Dance with Mother Earth" guided meditation. This is a moving meditation that should be done outdoors and, if possible, with bare feet for the deepest connection to Mother Earth. An audio version of this meditation is available on my website as a download at KamiGuildner.com/Firedancer.

Dance with Mother Earth Guided Meditation

Take a scan of your body right now. Do you notice tension anywhere? If so, take time to gently and playfully move these parts of your body. Tune out the noise of the world and feel the roots of expansiveness that exist beneath your feet and the skies that dance overhead. Invite the energetic flow of our earth to dance with you, to wrap around your heart. Tap the soles of your feet to the ground and breathe lightness into the busy pathways of your mind. Dance! Dance! Dance! And when I say dance, I mean dance. Putting your body into motion will set free some of the stickiness that makes its way into our bodies in the built-up tensions of a day. Skip and twirl. Set the firedancer in you free.

Lie down in the dirt and roll around. Then look up and notice the clouds and let the shapes take form. What do you see? Are the clouds still or are they in motion? Let the moment play with your soul. Breathe in the freshness of air. Then just notice. What has shifted in your body? Does anything feel different?

Chances are you've opened a pathway to your heart. A place and a space to be heard. Now close your eyes. Feel the rhythm of that space in nature. Feel the energy that emanates.

What is its essence? Invite that essence to comingle with your inner essence. To dance together in synchronicity. Notice what takes place in your body. Where do you feel this energy most? How do these energies comingle? Does it feel peaceful? Playful? Does inviting energy into your body change how you feel? This connection between you and the earth upon which you sit is sacred.

Reach out to the soil and take some into your hand. Again, notice its energies—its essence. Let those energies flow through you. Begin to intentionally comingle your energy with the earth's energy, and feel the interconnectedness of these energies dance within. Send these dancing energies out to the trees, the birds, all that is in nature around you. Connect this energy to other souls around the world. Intentionally share this gift of you. Open your heart to the world around you. Gift the rhythm, the good intention, the love, the peace. Simply send goodwill out into the world.

Raven Dancer

Brother Raven speaks from the spirit, messages beyond space and time. Secrets of health and harmony hidden in the midnight wings are felt in the wind. The palomino horse dances, its spirit filled with joy.

The magic intertwining energies of these sentient beings indicates change is at work. You are on the path you should be – listen to the messages inside. Watch for signs around you. There is something to know. Choices to be made. Your heart knows the right answers, so join in the dance of spirit and joy. Twirl. Leap. Flow. The path will unfold as it should.

5

Shining the Light on the Wonder That Is YOU!

"No story is worth telling without the twists and turns.
Make them count instead."
~Charlotte Eriksson

N ow that you've tuned into nature, we can begin to walk the path to reconnect to the Essence of You. What are your strengths? What are your passions? What do you value? Over the course of the following chapters, you will begin to reconnect with who you are at your very essence in order to answer these questions and more. The Essence of You is grounded in three fundamental pillars:

1. You have *gifts* to give to the world—strengths that will make a difference to those around you and talents that will

uplift you and others. This is not a study of limitations and weaknesses, but a focus on what works and creates value, along with an invitation to bring more of this into your world.

2. Your *values* continuously evolve. Over the course of your lifetime, some values change, while others—your soul values—are with you forever. Consider and weigh the most meaningful experiences in your life today. Consider which values are inherent in your soul.

3. Connecting with your *passion* is essential to your essence—and passion fuels big living in one's life. Passion provides us with the courage to step into worlds unknown and take risks that shake our inner core. It leads us down paths to open previously unimaginable doors.

The complex layers of your gifts, values, and passions weave an intricate cloth—a colorful fabric that is the Essence of You. Knowing yourself at this deep level provides a foundation that empowers you and gives you strength to take new action toward your calling—even if you don't have a clue what that might look like right now. Patience and perseverance will sustain you to unfold what is meant to open. It's hard work. It's deep work. And it will spiral the growth of possibilities in your life into meaning.

I believe the best way to weave this unique cloth of "you," and to start the discovery of the first pillar of strength, is to play in the stories of your life when you've been at your best—when you've been at the top of your game. There are clues in those stories: the ones that you tell over and over again, the stories that create a spark in your heart and set something afire deep in your soul, the stories that you remember most vividly. If you look closely, it's often a story where you were stretched to new limits, into capabilities that you didn't even know you had, and you grew and expanded and learned. These stories help you remember. You'll start to see patterns of the things you really excel at, of passions, of what really matters most to you. Looking into the archives of your stories reveals your most prolific talents and strengths.

Remembering My Stories

In the months that followed my father's death, I learned to slow down. I returned to my love of nature and found a new footing in life. Without the intense pace of meetings and travel I slowly tuned into my soul wisdom, giving myself permission to once again play in the things I loved.

I took time for lunches with friends. I wrote. I hiked. I grew deeply in love with the man who would be my future husband. I took time for my own growth. It was a gift I hadn't given myself permission to do throughout my entire life.

This is where my journey back to my essence began. For the first time in my life, I had space to ponder. I had time to dedicate to my own soul exploration. I had time to reconnect to a "me" that I'd lost along the way. Amidst that time filled with nature and people who really mattered in my life, my inward journey began. With this shift in my own state of being, the Universe once again delivered more gifts. The right coaches, teachers, and mentors began to show up in my life. And through this unfolding journey, I started to discover pieces of me that had been buried beneath the busy-ness.

One wise mentor and teacher, world-renowned author, Amanda Trosten Bloom, encouraged me to explore the most memorable stories in my life—to look beyond the surface into why those stories stood out. I was encouraged to be curious about the talents and passions I brought to those circumstances. As a result, I began to see patterns. I began to see threads that connected the times in my life where I'd had success and was able to notice the passions that lit me up. I was able to identify how I wove those into the fabric of me and added the deeply-rooted colors of my values. I discovered that what these elements created was beautiful. In the process, I fell in love with me again.

While during the majority of my career I had been a marketing exec, I began to realize that it wasn't marketing that moved me. What moved me were the projects and times when I was engaging with and developing people. My positive outlook on life was a gift that motivated others. And my responsible work ethic framed many of the successes that evolved in my life.

As I went deeper into the exploration of my stories, I realized that my intuition was strong. Looking back, I realized I had an intuitive sixth sense that had guided me into many positive life experiences—basically I had followed my gut. In contrast, there were other times in my life where my gut was telling me not do something … but I hadn't listened and proceeded anyway… and those proved to be wrong decisions. At the time, I hadn't believed or trusted those instincts. I was curious to find out what would happen if I started to tune into this intuitive gift.

The spiraling evolution of wisdom that unfolded in the year that followed my father's death would begin to lay the foundation for a dramatic life change. Reconnecting to the stories in my life, where I had my biggest successes and those that lit me on fire the most, was revealing. It reconnected me to my talents, my gifts, and my passions—to what really brought meaning to my life.

These discoveries fueled me. One by one, ideas of new possibilities blossomed. Some ideas stuck, and others gave way to new ideas. My creativity exploded. I let go of the doubt, the fear, and the insecurities that had come with being laid off. Suddenly I started to see the circumstances in my life as an opportunity for something more. The beautiful fabric of my essence was opening to a whole new world. The full vision for my future wasn't completely in focus as of yet, but the light was brighter and my heart leapt in anticipation for my entry into the unknown.

Remember Your Stories

What hidden messages lie in your stories? Let's start to examine the times in your life where you've felt on fire and excited about all that you were doing. There's a great likelihood that at those times you were deeply engaged with the aspects of yourself that you're the very best at—your gifts. You were probably doing things you were passionate about. And there's a very strong possibility that those times in your life where you were on fire and excited were in alignment with your values. Let's take a look.

Reflection

Consider the stories in your life that stand out most—the ones you tell most often, the ones that light you up as you recall them. Make a list of as many stories as you can, giving each one a name that reflects the experience. Are there any similarities or common threads amongst these stories? Just make note of this and save the list for the next chapter.

The Sun Dancer Within

Journey unto the center of you. There is knowing there. Reflect in the light that shines within and embrace the beauty of all that is around you. For this is your journey.

Each of the precious life experiences you have encountered along the way lead to this moment. The transformation that unfolds – and is unfolding before you – is as it should be. Live in this moment. Praise the gifts that you give unto this world. Give gratitude to life lessons that have come forth in your growth – in your own metamorphosis.

Embrace the souls of others who have joined in your journey. Consider how the mixing of your hearts, the culmination of your purposes and the flow of emotional energy brought new experiences, new lessons, new growth.

Let these life moments flourish within. Consider the connectedness between these circumstances and how they bring meaning to your own soul life. How do the dots connect? You have these answers within – it is the fabric of your own purpose. Your reason for being on this earth – at this time – in this place. Let this moment of transformation unfold as it should. Honor the knowing you have inside. Trust in what you hear. For it is the truth – your truth.

6

A Study of Your Strengths

"May what I do flow from me like a river, no forcing
and no holding back, the way it is with children."
~ Rainer Maria Rilke

The first pillar in the Essence of You is grounded in your Strengths—your naturally life-given gifts and talents. I want you to become intimately familiar with your strengths so that you can feed them, verbalize them, look for opportunities to work in them, and use them as a guiding light in important life decisions.

I'm not sure why we don't learn to do this when we're young. If the curriculum of our educational system helped each of us discover our gifts and talents early on, we might not go through our whole careers pushing and forcing avenues of opportunity, but rather, we would all be able to flow like rivers, as Rilke so eloquently wrote.

From the time we started grade school, through our college years, and into our working lives, we were told to focus on our weaknesses and grow from this place. From now on, I'm inviting you to shift that thinking. I don't care about your weaknesses! What I'm interested in is shining a light on your strengths and those unique gifts and talents that make you YOU. When you study what you do really well, nurture those gifts, and breathe life into those strengths, you get stronger and even better at them. And this is the place from which new possibilities begin to unfold in your life.

The same mentor who started my exploration of my life stories also introduced me to the Clifton StrengthsFinder® assessment by Gallup. This tool helped me put words to my gifts, and, more importantly, provided a framework to see myself in new light.

I learned that I: 1) am an arranger—someone who can see the way to connect the dots in complex situations—and that I am at my best in dynamic situations; 2) am fueled by positivity—I see the glass as half-full and never half-empty; 3) am an achiever—which really described my internal drive that moved my career and life; 4) am responsible—I have a deep-seated need to fulfill my commitments and take care of things in my life; 5) have belief as a driving force in my life—my commitment to my own core values drives my life choices and gives my life meaning.

Upon completion of this assessment, I started to see what

had gone astray in the latter years of my corporate career. While I certainly had an opportunity to work within my arranger, achiever, and responsibility talents, space to engage my positivity and belief talents was sorely lacking. My environment was fraught with negative battles, and I certainly wasn't doing work aligned to my values or anything that I passionately believed in or that mattered in a global world.

These five strengths identified by the Clifton StrengthsFinder® were magnified in the stories I had been exploring. For example, one story focused on how much I loved my international marketing work in my career—taking complex and diverse markets and finding ways to connect to those clients. I also told the story of the rebranding projects where I unified a very diverse suite of products for an overarching corporate brand. I was good at being able to connect the dots and find solutions amidst the chaos. This was the arranger in me magnified. These story connections embedded an even deeper knowing of my "Self."

Remembering the achiever in me, and the many stories that highlighted times in my life where my grit persevered, refueled my self-confidence at a time when I had taken quite a hit. Throughout that year of self-discovery, I continued to learn more about myself. One of the most dramatic discoveries that year was learning that I was a right-brain thinker. Once upon a time, I would have told you I was a solid left-brain woman. In my corporate years, I worked so extensively with my left-brain thinking that I regularly declared I wasn't the creative side of marketing. I relied on my creative counterparts to bring the marketing jazz to the table.

Imagine my surprise when I did a brain science assessment

that highlighted how I am more of a right-brain thinker. In fact, I learned that I am an eighty-seven percent right-brain thinker, and a thirteen percent left-brain thinker. It doesn't mean that I can't be good at working from my left-brain. In fact, I had become quite proficient at it. From the very early phases of my career, I trained my brain to work in the realms of numbers and logic. In the early eighties, I was an early user of Lotus 1-2-3, one of the first spreadsheet programs. For several years, I ran economic reports on oil and gas properties and reserves, teaching me about the time cost of money. I could tell you how oil was extracted from the earth and how gas was processed. As a VP of marketing, even my finance partners were in awe of my complex spreadsheets that rolled up gigantic fifty-plus tabbed spreadsheets.

All this left-brained thinking was truly a learned skill for me. It had been a circumstantial learning path that propelled me in my career. My opportunistic drive saw an organizational need and gap, so I stepped into the doors that opened.

But left-brain thinking didn't fill me up. The highly procedural work depleted me, and I'd wake up in the middle of the night pushing numbers in my head. After working on big projects like these, I'd often need days to recover.

That brain science assessment also highlighted my preference for big-picture thinking and social experiences, for my need to be around people. Again, I could see more patterns.

The assessment also brought light to my intuitive capabilities. I had denied my intuition for most of my adult life. I had great intuition about ideas—what would work and what wouldn't. My gut instinct about people in my life was generally right, but I didn't trust it. I even remember having a boss, who I didn't really favor, tell me that my intuition didn't matter. "It is all about the metrics," he would say. It was no wonder I had shut down this aspect of myself.

So often when I first meet a new client, I quickly learn that they've come through some pretty rough situations. Perhaps they got laid off from their job or experienced a failed partnership or marriage or lost a promotion. Sometimes they come to me actually wishing that some of these changes would happen. In any case, their perception of their personal gifts are often skewed and even lost amidst the chaos and crisis that have occurred. They may think that their past successes were a mere façade.

One of my clients, Joe, had a successful twenty-plus-year career in a consulting firm when his company was acquired by a mega-billion dollar global firm. In our first meeting together, he told me about his recent review in which his new boss declared to him that he wasn't a good leader. This statement shook Joe's world. He'd been a leader of a high-producing team of engineers for many years. They'd been profitable and results-driven, and his team members were loyal and respected him. Equally important, his customer satisfaction levels were extremely high.

Now, if we would have dug right into the realm of goal setting and action steps in order to focus on the weakness of not leading well, we would have missed an important discovery. Instead, we dug into the highlight stories of Joe's career that stood out the most to him. He shared the details of the stories, of what moved him, who was involved, the situations, and the results. I watched for the sparks in each story—the kind of moments where he lit up around certain details. These spark moments started to shine a light on what moved Joe and where he felt the greatest empowerment.

At the same time, we did a Syzygy 360° Strengths Profile™ on Joe by having a group of Joe's colleagues recall stories where they'd seen him at his best. They were asked: "Tell me about another time when you experienced me at my best. What unique gifts, abilities, strengths, and qualities of character did I display?" As the feedback started to come in, Joe suddenly had new insights. He learned that his coworkers, colleagues, employees, and personal connections all independently identified leadership as Joe's top strength. In fact, without any prompting, they admitted that they'd follow his leadership anywhere.

Ultimately, Joe was able to really shine a light on the types of leadership he was best at and the kind of environment in which he would flourish. The big company environment wasn't a fit, but ultimately he became the president of a small engineering consultancy. And guess what? Many of the people he knew followed him there—both employees and clients!

Your Journey to You

What hidden messages lie in your stories? Start to examine the times in your life where you've felt on fire and excited about all you were doing. There's a great likelihood you were deeply engaged with the aspects of yourself that you're the very best at— your gifts, talents, and strengths. You were probably doing things you were passionate about. And there's a very strong possibility that all of these were aligned to your values. Let's take a look.

Reflection

1. Write the story about a peak experience you've had in your life. It may have been a time when you felt most alive, most involved, or most excited about what you were involved in. What made it an exciting experience? Who was involved? What feelings did you have? Write the story in detail.

    a. After you've written the story, read through it and consider: "What strengths, gifts, and talents did I exhibit and lean into in this situation?" Write down five strengths, gifts, and talents that you identified in this situation.

    b. Repeat this exercise with a second and third peak experience, perhaps from different areas of your life. What do you notice? Are there similarities in your gifts between the stories? Or are you identifying additional strengths? Write down as many personal strengths as you can identify.

c. Circle the top five strengths that you exhibit when you're at your best. Write these down.

2. I encourage you to invite eight to ten people across all walks of your life to respond to the following questions in the Syzygy 360° Strengths Profile™ Survey. For example, invite an employer, an employee or colleague, a neighbor, a special relative, a spouse, or someone with whom you served on a committee or in a volunteer situation. Explain to them that this is part of your journey to understand your very essence and that their feedback will provide valuable insights into *who you are* at your very core. Thank them in gratitude for their time and thoughtfulness.

360° Strengths Profile™ Survey

Everyone has unique gifts, talents, and strengths that, when expressed, bring them joy and fulfillment and enable them to make a meaningful contribution to the world. These same gifts, when brought forth in relationships, teams, communities, and organizations, can inspire others and enable their greatest contributions. Inspired life emerges more readily when people know their unique gifts. I would like to learn what you see as my unique gifts, talents and strengths.

▲ Tell me about a time when you experienced me at my best. What was the situation? Who else was involved?

▲ What unique gifts, abilities, and strengths—values, beliefs, commitments, qualities of character, knowledge, skills, or practices—did I display?

▲ What was the result of my involvement in this situation?

▲ Based on this experience, what positive life potential do you see in me that I may not yet see in myself or fully acknowledge?

The gift of a response to these questions will provide insights into your strengths that you might not have even acknowledged in your own stories. As you read through the responses that are returned to you, a pattern will most likely develop. People who know you from different areas of your life will often identify the very same theme or strength. Look for the synchronicities and then identify the top five strengths that evolved from your acquaintances.

3. On page 219, you will find an Essence of You diagram that you're going to develop. Write your five strengths from your 360° Strengths Profile™ feedback on your Essence of You diagram. Also add your top five strengths related to your own peak experience story from the first reflection above. You have begun your exploration of who you are at your very core. Congratulations!

4. Answer the following question: At my best I am … (list

five adjectives). Then translate these to your Essence of
You diagram.

1.

2.

3.

4.

5.

There are many online self-assessments that can help you
identify unique gifts. My favorite is the Clifton StrengthsFinder
assessment. Take the online test of your top strengths at https://
www.gallupstrengthscenter.com/ and add these to your Essence
of You diagram.

Other good online assessments that can provide good insights into who you are at your best include:

▲ Disc Personality Assessment:
   http://discpersonalitytesting.com/
▲ Enneagram:
   https://www.enneagramworldwide.com/test
▲ Emergenetics:
   https://www.emergenetics.com/take_a_profile.html

As you read through these various profiles, remember to focus your study on your strengths, not your weaknesses. Many
assessments will provide details into your strengths and weaknesses. While understanding your weaknesses can be useful,
I want you to practice shining a light on your strengths. Get
into the habit of spending four times as much focus on your
strengths in whatever form of feedback you receive. This will
fuel and shape your journey aligned to what you're great at!

Your Gift

In a misty dawn, bathed in golden light – bestow a gift – the gift of you. Open your heart with authenticity and listen. Hear the stories of others. And listen yet deeper.

Extend your hands – as a friend, a confidante, a partner. Share in your abundance, share in your support. Is it kindness that you can provide? Is it a helping hand?

Feel the golden energy flow of caring – from you to another, from the universe to all. With intention, add to the beauty of this golden light. Offer yourself unto this world. Make a difference in the life of another.

7

Values – Your
Soul's Bedrock

Your values will constantly shapeshift throughout your entire life. What you valued as a twenty-year-old is different than what you will value as a fifty-year-old. As a young adult, your values were probably shaped by your parents' values and early childhood experiences. Then you discovered freedom of choice, and you began to formulate your own value patterns.

Your early values guide your choices—where you go to school, the jobs you take, the friends you choose to spend time with. And those choices bring a world of experiences to your journey. Experiences guide and maneuver your value system. Children, roles, cultures, key people in your life all continue the shapeshifting journey.

And while many of our values shapeshift and evolve with our life experiences, there are some values that are simply an intricate piece of who we are. Perhaps we were born with these values meant to serve our journey in this lifetime. Or perhaps we were born into the environment and families that nurtured these values. I'm not certain. But in either case, they are part of our soul. These are your soul values. These deeply ingrained values never leave us. They are the ones that fill us up when we're depleted. And if we leave them behind, our soul has a deep longing for them.

For example, I believe the need to be in nature is a personal value that I was born with—something key to my soul journey. Is it happenstance that I was born into a family where this value was nurtured and encouraged? I don't think so. It's all part of the Universe's grand plan for my life.

Both shapeshifting values and soul values can get lost amidst the noise and craziness of life. Both are important to understand. Most of us, however, don't stop to tune into our values as a regular practice. We get caught up in the flow of our surroundings and lose sight of our own value systems.

It's a societal dilemma. We live busy lives. We feel stretched thin. We continually negotiate demands on time and craziness of schedules with back-to-back meetings that never end. We find our work lives extending into the evenings of each weekday and into our weekends. It's almost as if our busy-ness spills into every waking hour, minute, and second. Who has time to stop and notice whether they've lost sight of what they once valued? In the midst of our busy-ness, understanding what those values are or how they've changed isn't as important as it once was—we simply don't have time to contemplate our values.

I believe losing touch with our values is often the driving force behind that calling we get, that urging that sounds like, "I want something more in my life, but I don't know what it is." This is the theme that makes my coaching business go round. Sometimes it's shapeshifting values that are the driving force— kids have grown up and life is just different than it was ten or fifteen years ago. At other times, it's soul values that have not been nurtured for years. Oftentimes, it's both. It really doesn't matter which type of values are out of balance in your life. What matters is whether, right now in this time and place, you've lost alignment to what's most important in your life. Tuning into values provides a giant clue as to *what* is calling within, into your longing for something more.

The signposts I was getting before I transformed my journey from the corporate world were clues that my values had shifted. My son had grown up, I'd put many years of intense focus on a career that had treated me well, and I had discovered the sweet taste of success and financial rewards that had come my way. The internal whispers of my soul helped me know that something was missing.

Yet, for a long time, I hadn't stopped to consider what brought meaning to my world. In the days that followed my father's death, I retreated to the paths through the woods around my home and was drawn to the whispers of the trees. I took quiet time in my barn. I listened.

In the early morning daylight of my barn, I watched a nest of baby sparrows as they took their first flight. One by one, they each took a fateful leap into the world from the safe ledge that had been their whole world. As the first bird took flight, she cautiously landed on a ledge on the opposite side of the aisle, her feet grasping tightly. Filled with the adrenaline that got her to the new spot, she chirped loudly, "Did you see me? Did you see me?" to her brothers and sisters who were still sitting safely in their childhood home.

Swirling in circles, momma and daddy bird cheered the brave young bird on and then returned to the remaining young birds in the nest. They chirped and rapidly swirled around the nest, "You can do it, yes, come on, you can do it." Momma bird returned to the brave bird, and together they launched themselves to a fence line outside the safe confines of the barn, leaving daddy bird to cheer and lead the remaining birds, one by one, into flight.

As I watched this family affair unfold, I realized I hadn't taken this kind of time to observe nature in a very long time. It had been quite a while since I really just stopped and watched the wonderment of nature. My father's death stopped my world and changed the whole perspective of what was important in my life and in life in general. As I left the barn, I sat down and wrote the following poem. It was a healing piece filled with gratitude for the man who raised me.

To My Father: You Taught Me

You taught me how to ride a horse
and that mountains clear your mind.
You taught me that the love of family
can make the world shine.

You taught me that a favorite rock
lets you talk to God.
You taught me to care for animals
and to keep my horses shod.

You taught me how to change a tire
and the oil – and with that how to cuss.
You taught me how to build a box,
sanded smooth and just.

You taught me to never let the
'sons of bitches' get me down and
to hold my head up high.

You taught me that friends are for keeping
– they'll bring you laughter
when things go a'righ.

You taught me to not roll my eyes at you
– it really made you really mad.
You taught me to not fight with you
– it really made you really sad.

You taught me how to forgive,
when things weren't eye-to-eye.
You taught me that love ranks
all and is the holding tie.

You taught me to stand up for what I believe is right.
You taught me I can do anything –
through thick or thin or plight.

You taught me how to raise my son –
of that I'm proud and true.
You taught him to hunt, smoke cigars,
drink whiskey – but many life lessons too.

You taught me how to love a spouse
with your very deepest core.
You taught me that I want the same for me
– who could ask for more?

You taught me to bear the pain – never with a fuss.
You taught me that hugs, smiles and laughter
will make a bad day turn flush.

You taught me that it hurts so much now you've gone away.
You taught me that even with all our time,
I still have things to say.

You're teaching me to look for you in the signs of nature –
the birds, the sunset, the breeze.

You're teaching me I can still talk to you even in the leaves.

So I'll watch for signs my dear father,
and I will tell you about my day.
I'll tell you that I miss you and whatever else I need to say.
You've been my greatest teacher
and helped me become me.

I'll miss you Daddy.
I love you.
Kami

When I wrote this poem, I suddenly realized how discon-nected I had become from some of these life lessons. He had entrenched these into me at such an early age, and although I still held them dearly, there was little evidence of them in my current life. Many of these soul values were completely absent, yet they were an inherent part of me. This realization was one of my early clues to what was missing in my life.

It's true that our values shift over time. Some of the values we have in our twenties and thirties are often not the same as the ones we will have when we're in our fifties and sixties. Yet there are some that our soul will long for if we leave them be-hind—our soul values. That is what I discovered when I wrote that poem. There were places in me that were calling to be nur-tured and to be realigned into balance. It was from this knowing that I changed and began to make new choices.

When you reconnect with all that is meaningful in your life and ask yourself the question, "What is most important to me?" the choices you make each day come into a new light.

One of my clients, a senior vice president in a Fortune 100 company, was traveling to NYC from Colorado every week for work. Despite holding a very prestigious role, she knew something needed to shift. Her inner wisdom was calling out to her—she was exhausted, she missed her family, and she was having all the health signposts that something needed to change.

She was also being put into some compromising positions in her role, which bordered on breaking her personal integrity boundaries. In a precipitous moment, she quit—after listening to her own inner voice that told her it just wasn't the right place for her to be.

As we worked together, she got really clear about her values and began to realize just why that role had been wrong for her on so many levels. Her number one work-related value was location. Not far behind that were family, integrity, and honesty. New to her discovery was a knowing that she wanted to help others and have moral fulfillment in her work.

With this deeper understanding of what was important to her, she decided it was time to step into work that brought her extensive business background into making a difference for others. Today, she sits on several boards of nonprofits for which she has a passion. She also owns her own business coaching and consulting company, where she helps others create successful businesses.

Her spiraling roadmap enabled her to channel her life stories and experiences into more meaningful work. The deeper understanding of what was most important to her from a value perspective helped guide her choices. Her journey certainly didn't follow a straight line. It took exploration, being present and intentional, trying things on for size, and letting the Universe deliver its own style of yeses and nos. Her journey became grounded in a deeper understanding of who she was at her essence and what mattered to her. In the journey between leaving one job and starting her company, job opportunities came and went. Some she chose to leave behind and others just weren't meant to be. In the end, her pathway opened up in the way she was meant to travel.

At first glance, it appeared risky and scary to start her own company, for she had always lived in the corporate world. But the signposts kept leading her to her destination. She listened, knowing that she had to make a difference in her work. She got all the right yeses that gave her the courage to say yes to her Self. Today, she loves the work she does—work that is aligned to her top values of location, integrity, work-life balance, family, moral fulfilment, and the need to help others. She shaped her world by choice.

Reflection

Over the course of my work with clients, I have never run into two people who had the same exact values. Some people lead with family, others with solving challenging problems or job tranquility. Others want to work on the frontiers of knowledge or engage their creative capabilities, while others are seeking advancement opportunities or higher earnings. There are so many choices to consider. The values that you embody today are yours alone, and they will guide you as you contemplate what you do and don't want. Consider the things that you value deeply. What matters most to you?

1. From the following list of values, circle your top 20 values in your life today. Don't overthink the exercise; merely go with your first instinct.

Abundant Mindset	Dependability	Honesty	Power
Accomplishment	Diversity	& Integrity	Professionalism
Achievement	Effectiveness	Independence	Public Contact
Advancement	Efficiency	Influence Others	Recognition
Adventure	Empowerment	Innovation	Risk Taking
Ambition	Excellence	Knowledge	Safety
Autonomy	Expressiveness	Leadership	Spirituality
Beauty	Fairness	Learning	Spontaneity
Being the Best	Family	Location	Stability
Calmness	Fast Pace	Love	Status
Change & Variety	Flexibility	Loyalty	Structure and
Collaboration	Friendships	Making Decisions	Predictability
Community	Fun & Humor	Making a	Teamwork
Compassion	Generosity	difference	Time Freedom
Competence	Grace	Meaning	Tradition
Competition	Happiness	Passion	Trust
Connection	Hard work	Peace &	Working with
to Nature	Harmony	Tranquility	Challenges
Creativity	Health	Performance	Work-Life Balance
Delight in Life	High Earnings	Personal Growth	

As you look at your top 20, consider if there are any values you've held consistently your whole life—your soul values. Put a star next to your soul values. Finally, review your top 20 list once more, and put a check mark next to your top 10 values today. Transfer these 10 values to the Essence of You Diagram, starring any that are soul values.

2. Role Models: Think about three role models. Describe the values they appear to live by. Journal about the things you admire in each person. Reflect on how you live (or don't live) those same values. How might you incorporate more of those values into your own life?

3. Take a walk in nature and find a quiet spot to journal on the things you value most today in your life. As you sit quietly, feel into your heart. Listen. She will speak to you if you tune in. Jot down random words that come forth from this space. Notice what is happening around you in nature and let nature be your guide. Feel into the flow.

4. Consider the question: "What would your seventy-year-old self tell you today?" This is a powerful exercise to listen to your inner wisdom. Close your eyes and let her speak to you. Listen deeply with your heart. Record in your journal everything she reveals to you.

Balance

The horse pauses from a drink and looks as the moon grows darker. The eclipse casts its glow.

The eclipse is created through alignment of the celestial bodies – it is a syzygy. It is time to create alignment in your life with a balance of spirit, body, mind and emotion. Pause in your day to take wonder in your life, to honor and give gratitude for the good. Hold dear to your heart all that is right and let the light of goodness lead your way.

8

Finding the Passion
in Your World

"There is some kiss we want with our whole lives. The touch of spirit on the body. Sea water begs the pearl to break its shell and the lily, how passionately It needs some wild darling. At night, I open the window and ask the moon to come and press its face to mine. Breathe into me. Close the language door and open the love window."
~ Rumi

For as long as I can remember, I've had a passionate soul. As a little girl, I greeted my horse each day with, "Good morning love." My passion for my family and friends beats wildly and guides the circles of my life. I long for adventure and play—whether it's hiking a mountain, traveling to far-off places, or meeting interesting people in new cultures.

I can feel passion running through my veins. The exhilaration feeds my soul. When one of my clients gets a major aha moment, my body celebrates in passion for work that I love.

In my days when I was single, the word passion was always prominent in my online dating profile titles, "SWF, Passionate about Life, Seeks Fun-Loving Handsome Man." Yes, passion is an intricate thread of my very fabric.

In fact, it's an intricate thread of everyone's fabric. The language of passion is felt through our whole body. When Rumi wrote, "Close the language door," he was inviting us to tune into the experience of the moment and feel it. I invite you to step out on the daring edge of feeling your passions. There's fire here. There's exhilaration. And there's vulnerability. This vulnerability can be raw. Yet, it is this very rawness that lets you live fully into your potential. When you take the courage to live into your passions and ultimately into your life potential, you will find deep meaning in life. You will awaken the firedancer within you.

My Journey into Living My Passion

It took me seventeen months from the day I left my corporate job to the day I discovered my new path. The synchronistic gift for me was that these seventeen months occurred during the downward spiraling economy that began that fall of 2008.

As the stock market dropped to new lows and unemployment to new highs, there were no jobs to be found, leaving me with plenty of time to think. The pieces had started to formulate, yet I hadn't quite put them all together.

In late October 2009, the pieces began to fall into place. It had already snowed a foot that day when an email came from

Anna, a horse trainer friend I had once worked with. When I met her several years before, I felt an instant connection to her energy. You know, it's the kind that you want to have in your life—optimistic, insightful, intuitive. I tend to pay attention to this type of energy and often am humored how these people will re-enter my life years later at a very opportune time. This was one of those days—one of those moments.

Anna's email that day was promoting a podcast with a woman named Lisa.

"Sit down for an hour with Lisa for an inspiring conversation about nothing less than how to listen to that inner voice and guide your life toward the extraordinary adventure of living an enlightened, inspired, and fulfilling life. Discover the life you're meant to live and how to open up and realize your destiny."

With a sudden spark, I felt my journey deepen. Many words in the email jumped out at me: "extraordinary adventure ...," "living an enlightened, inspired and fulfilling life ...," "realize your destiny ..." Who is Lisa? So I turned to Google. As I reached her website, I was drawn in by the photos of horses. Yet, her work was about personal growth. I was intrigued. Horses and personal growth—how do they relate?

Looking at the pictures of the people and the horses, I could see connections. There was something about the horse presence that prompted an interesting link. And then the site prompted, "Want to learn more about the power of unexpected connections?"

"Yes!" I said out loud and quickly entered my contact details.

Lisa reached out to me within minutes, and soon we had

a phone appointment set up for later that morning. Digging deeper on Google, I discovered that Lisa worked with horses to help people discover their dreams. How cool is that!?! I wasn't sure what to expect from our call, but the unearthing of emotions that came about in a one-hour phone conversation was certainly not part of my expectations.

Lisa listened patiently as I shared the stories of my soul-searching journey and described the crossroads at which I had arrived. I told her that none of my options felt quite right—perhaps I hadn't found a missing piece of my puzzle that would make this all clear. With a simple question, Lisa tapped into the heart of it: "What are your passions?"

Passion—a word that had always spoken to me. Yet, it was an energy I'd lost in my last years of working in the corporate grind. Work had been about something else—progress, growth, more from less, delivery. The passion had been gone and I knew it.

Surprisingly, I found myself in tears. What fears are holding me back? Afraid of failure perhaps? Was I as successful as I had believed? Or was it all a facade? Why can't I find a place to belong?

Lisa was patient, letting me find words that I wasn't sure were even there. The emotions were raw, and she just allowed them to be, asking me to tune in and experience my body. "What do you feel?" she asked. I noticed a pit in my stomach. Yet, when she asked me to describe my fears, this pit released and gently flowed from my body—a beautiful gift.

When we were done, Lisa recommended I take the day—this day of quiet snowfall—to just be. To ponder. She suggested that I go to the barn and just breathe in my horse's breath and see what came to me. So, with emotions exposed, I did just that. My paint mare, Sugaree, seemed to call to me, wanting to share in the moment. She stood patiently as I breathed in her warm, wet breath on that frosty day. Sugaree offered trust, a willingness to see where this whole experience was leading. After a few moments, I turned my back to her back and rested my head upon her shoulder, soaking in her good energy. There is a huge energy that encompasses you in a horse's presence. I allowed it to fill my nooks and crannies, to flow through my veins, to calm and soothe me.

When I returned to the house, I took out my journal and pen and had a hard time keeping up with the pace of my mind. The bared emotions that came forth also brought new visions of what could be. I found a renewed commitment to align to my authentic self that had somehow been misplaced along the way. I began uncovering a path to me.

They say that following your passion leads to an extraordinary life. As I began to explore the possibilities, all of the pieces of the puzzle I had diligently uncovered over the prior seventeen months seemed to drop perfectly into place. It was such an "Aha!" moment that I sat wondering, *How did I not see this path before?*

There in front of me was a way that I could connect horses and my professional past. As I explored how other people were successfully coaching leaders and teams with horses in such ways that I had never even thought of previously, my enthusiasm soared. I could do this! I would be combining all of my most passionate of passions together. It was extraordinary in the most extraordinary way!

What followed was an amazing flow of new people who came into my life and grounded these new ideas. Opening my heart to new possibilities was the first step—and it certainly worked for me. Within the week, I had met a dozen contacts—people began to drop into my life from the most unexpected places. It seemed the Universe had shifted and the gifts were bountiful. It was synchronicity at its best. The wisdom that came forth from Sugaree's warm breath on that wintry day—the wisdom that let all of my puzzle pieces fall into place—was the inception of my newfound understanding of the gift of horse in my life.

This was an epiphany moment that I will remember forever. It shaped my life journey, leading me away from a corporate career that I never thought I'd leave, to finding courage to step into an unknown. I could feel in my very core that this was the right path for me—that magnetic pull led me with a vigorous draw I'd never before felt. There was such drive and assuredness I was on the right path, that even my always supportive mother's comments, "You're going to do what? (long pause) … I hope that works … (even longer pause)…" didn't faze me. Something inside told me this was indeed my right path.

A sure sign that I'd stepped onto the right path was how doors started to open in all directions. New people walked into my life who took me deeper into that journey. I started noticing others doing the kind of work that I hadn't even known about before. Ideal clients showed up who needed my help. Ideas came like crazy. The general pace of my journey accelerated and broadened my world.

How was it that I found clarity at that time, after seventeen months of seeking and searching? It was because this was the catalyst moment. It had been preceded by quiet pause and massive self-exploration. My personal growth journey over those seventeen months had been deep and wide. I had to pause in my life questions and stories before this epiphany could reveal itself to me. That moment in the barn defined a significant shift in my future. My future would incorporate horses and nature and people. Before that moment, I wasn't seeing the possibilities of how these elements in my life could fit together. It was in this epiphany event—this catalyst moment—that my puzzle pieces fell into place in a magical, mystical way. There was a deep knowing that "this is it." No longer were there multiple paths I could take—it just became a resounding YES for me to proceed. From that moment my journey continued to spiral within its expanding pathway, evolving from this newfound discovery. The synchronicity of the email message from Anna that October day started a wave of changes that continue even today. This is the magic of our life ride.

Our lives are filled with magical and mystical moments that we often miss amidst the noise. If we're moving at a pace that leaves no space to recognize these moments, we blow past the possibilities that present themselves.

Yet, every experience in our life builds upon the ones that came before. When you step into ideas that light up your curiosity and you start to ask yourself, "What if …" pay attention and tune in. Take time to engage in your passions. In those passions, I invite you to close the language door that dominates most people's lives and listen for deeper guidance—the kind I found that day with Sugaree in the barn. The kind that you might find on a hike through the woods or by splashing in the waves of the sea.

Finding the Passion in Your Stories

Is it no surprise that your passions can be discovered in your life stories? I want you to open the love window of your life and glimpse into the times that you have felt the deepest passions, the strongest pulsations. That place you feel most alive.

For some reason, passion is an area where I see the most resistance. There are all kinds of declarations of resistance, such as, "I can't make a living doing this," or "I don't have enough time." Or perhaps it's a simple, "I don't know where to start." At this point, I'm only asking you to be curious—to explore what moves you.

The reality is: you don't have to make a living with your passions. You may or may not want to pursue your passions as your profession. You merely need to make time for them. The reality is if you are partaking in things that light you up, your body and mind are more open to letting your inner creativity play and live. Inspiration is alive in your heart, and curiosity around what might be thrives. For instance, if you are passionate about music, take time for music. If you are a musician, find people to play with. If you enjoy listening to music, go to a concert or recital. Creating space for passion changes people's worlds.

This journey you're on is not a straight line. It is life experiences that fuel the place you're at today and the place you're going tomorrow. If your life experiences are passion-driven, your spiraling journey will be enriched and accelerated into even more meaningful experiences. It's merely the law of nature. If you're bored and living a life of doldrums, your spiraling journey slows to a snail's pace and what unfolds beyond that is merely more mundane existence. When you feed your journey with passion, your life experiences become colorful and inspiring.

What I see with my clients, once they step into this realm of passion-living, are the new "what-if" scenarios that begin to spark.

One of my clients, Stephanie, came to work with me after she had just sold her very successful marketing firm. For the first time in her adult life, she was questioning her career path. She'd lost her passion for the work she did and felt like she was missing something important in her life. She shared, "It can be very overwhelming to not have a handle on where you want to go and what you want to do, especially if your self-image has been tightly tied to your profession in the past."

One of her early discoveries in her passion work was remembering how much she loved art. In fact, that was the original reason she had chosen her pathway into marketing. But in the course of her very lucrative career she had stopped "doing art."

Stephanie's awareness that art was missing in her life led to the assignment, "go play in your art." What spawned from that assignment was an artistic journey. Stephanie created a mandala that represented her learnings and discoveries. She was once again working in her craft, and with this experience came new thinking for Stephanie. She felt her own healing. She faced her fears head on. She got clear about the things she wanted in her life.

The fire generated from her work helped her realize that she had other gifts to give to the world. Stephanie had great compassion for people and wanted to help others. She went back to school to pursue a psychology degree and explored the specialized field of art therapy, which would require an additional master's degree. She loved the concept of applying her love for art in the world and was especially intrigued with how art therapy could help veterans.

As she neared the completion of her psychology degree, with acceptance letters from multiple universities across the nation for art therapy programs, she began to feel some inner hesitation toward continuing her education in art therapy. There was a $70,000 price tag associated with completing the program, and the starting salaries for art therapists was small compared to her marketing world salary. After a great deal of inner contemplation, Stephanie made a much labored decision not to pursue this specialized art therapy degree.

Yet, she questioned her judgment and wondered if she had made the right decision. Although she wondered if she was letting people down who had been cheering her through the process, her instincts told her it wasn't the right thing for her ... and she listened to those internal messages. Slowing down and taking the time to play in her art had taught her to reconnect and trust those instincts.

In the meantime, other doors opened. Old colleagues from the marketing world reached out to her. They were looking for someone to work with them on some big strategic marketing projects—someone with a background in psychology. As a result, she re-entered the world of marketing and advertising with a different focus—and she found a renewed sense of passion for the work that she was doing. She loved the people and she loved the projects. What was different this time was that Stephanie continued to play in her art on a very regular basis—she made it a priority in her life. Her soul was happy.

But the story doesn't end there. One evening Stephanie attended an event at an art gallery, with no intention of buying art. However, there was a picture of a llama that caught her eye. She couldn't stay away from it all evening. She had no idea why—she didn't have a huge love of llamas—but the picture kept calling to her. She returned to it many times over the course of the evening. Finally, as the night neared a close, she decided to listen to her heart and bought the piece. When she went to hang the piece in its newfound place in her home, she turned it over and noticed a small tag on the back. The tag indicated that the proceeds from the sale of this painting were going to the nonprofit Art of War—helping veterans through art.

Suddenly, it dawned on her that there were other pathways for Stephanie to combine her love of art, help others, and utilize her strategic marketing experience. Stephanie decided to find a nonprofit board to get engaged with, similar to Art of War. Her signpost came in the form of a painting that evening. It helped her see how she could incorporate a main passion in a different direction.

In reflecting upon this journey with me, Stephanie shared, "It took so much courage to listen to my inner voice that told me not to pursue the advanced degree. But I knew it wasn't the right choice for me. It took that painting for me to see ways that my passions could come together."

Stephanie's biggest lesson has been that things don't always look exactly like you thought they would. In her wisdom, she shared, "Live where life is taking you and you will be grateful for the joy that comes your way." She found this journey by opening up her heart, learning to slow down, and exploring her passions. She found this journey by engaging in her passion and making it part of her exploration. This work helped her learn to listen to her inner wisdom and pay attention to the signposts that came into her life.

Passion lights up our soul. It helps us see, feel, and act in authentic ways that reveal who we are. It can guide our decisions and awaken something deep within us. It feeds our spiraling firedancer journey.

Whether your future involves working in your passion or not, awakening the passions in your life will bring new life to your world. It begins with curiosity. Curiosity spawns innovation and new ideas. Being curious about the question, "What if I brought more of what I love to do into my days?" along with Stephanie's awakened exploration of art fueled the possibilities that she saw before her. It opened up a flowing energy of new ideas. I invite you to embrace your inner curiosity and let ideas come without judgment.

There are no bad ideas in this early phase of discovery. So, as you start to play in your own themes of passion, be prepared for your own creativity to flow. New ideas and "what if" scenarios may present themselves. Be curious! Begin to keep an idea log of things you might do in the future and set aside your inner critic that shuts this creative process down. Turn off the naysaying disclaimers of "there's no way," "there's not enough time/money/resources," or any other ways that you might start to focus on the "how." There's a time and a place for that down the road. For now, just be curious with a "what if."

The fire of passion lives within you. It's not an external exercise. Give yourself space and time to engage your heart and light the spark within. This is what will lead you to starting the flame of passion that can't be put out.

Reflection

I invite you to play in the following passion exercise to tune into the heart of your passions. Head out for a walk in your favorite place in nature and start considering all the times in your life where you've felt this passion pulsation—a physical vibrant sensation beating through your veins—as a child … in your career … in your life. Then find a place that calls to you and sit down and capture your passions in the following areas. Record them in your journal.

- ▲ Childhood: Open the love window to when you were a child. Recall experiences that stand out most to you— the ones where you felt the deepest passions, the strongest pulsations, the most alive. What activities did you love? Who were the people that moved you? What made your heart skip?
- ▲ Career: Open the love window of your career. Recall when you felt the deepest passions, the strongest pulsations, the most alive. What activities did you love? Who were the people that moved you? What made your heart skip?
- ▲ Life: Open the love window of your life. Recall when you felt the deepest passions, the strongest pulsations, the most alive. What activities did you love? Who were the people that moved you? What made your heart skip?

Now you get to paint the threads that bind! Pull out a set of colored pencils or highlighters. Find the threads of similarity that exist in the stories that you recall. Circle them. Link them. Are there themes of commonality that show up? Identify four to five threads of your passion fabric and list them.

1.

2.

3.

4.

5.

Transcribe your passion threads to your Essence of You diagram. Do you see a picture of you starting to take shape in this Essence of You diagram? Your passion threads bring light into your world and make you feel alive at your very core. When you weave these threads into your life you are happy. Content. And very much alive!

The Fire of Passion

In passion, our hearts lead the way – making the impossible, possible. With light and brilliance abound, passion unleashes your soul's deepest desires.

Be fully in love with your world today. Live wildly in your passions. Allow your body to dance freely to the beautiful, spiraling and uplifting energy that passion creates. The colors of passion stream from your world to others, gifting new possibilities in their paths as well as your own, for passion is contagious.

This exponentially growing and spiraling flow of energy makes our world a better place. It shifts the global consciousness toward empowerment and fulfillment – making a difference to many.

And it starts with you today. Merely play in your passion – whatever it may be!

9

Stepping into the
Essence of You

"Can words describe the fragrance
of the very breath of spring?"
~ Neltje Blanchan

Such a journey you've started. With a deeper connection into nature you are surely feeling a lighter awareness of your very soul. The colorful threads of your personal gifts and strengths have begun to weave into the very fabric that is you. Your passion threads sparkle against the foundation of your deep values. Are you starting to see the picture that is unfolding?

Now is the time to relish in the discovery that depicts the Essence of You. Let's look more deeply at the meaning behind the word *essence*.

Essence: 1. All that makes a person who they are, their nature. 2. An indispensable quality. 3. An extract of something or someone, containing all of its important qualities in concentrated form.

I want to point out that you have led an extraordinary life already. And you've led this extraordinary life because it's yours and yours alone. What is it about *you* that has contributed to this journey? What is it about *you* that will shape your future into an even more extraordinary life? Tap into the positive and grounded realities of what makes *you* special to find the answers. This is your essence. It has been with you since the beginning and will be with you throughout your life.

Are you ready to paint the vision of who you are at your very core and in all your concentrated form? You're now going to begin to write an Essence of You statement—a short two- to four-sentence compilation of who you are at your very core. Look at the words that have come forth in the Essence of You diagram. These are components of who you are. Embrace each word. Celebrate the wonder that is you. Circle and highlight the words that stand out most to you. Recall your stories that ignited your heart. Then write a few sentences that encapsulate who you are at your very core.

Afterwards, simply sit on it—hang it on your mirror and read what you wrote out loud every day for a whole week. Play in the words. Wordsmith it if you feel compelled. Look over your Essence of You diagram and consider whether there are any missing key components in the words you've chosen. Meditate on it. If words pop into your head, consider if they belong there.

Share it with a friend and tell them what you've discovered that is unique and beautiful about you. Live into it with peaceful and loving intent, and let it be born into existence naturally. Essence statements are not born overnight. It takes time—even weeks—and introspection. Be gentle with yourself and play in it until you love it. Trust that it will unfold. When your Essence of You statement is done, you'll simply know. You'll love the carefully chosen words. It will resonate in your heart.

I love when clients discover their essence. Here's a sampling of some of the favorites that have come forth over the years.

▲ I am Heart of a Lion! What I do must matter. I am honest, hardworking, passionate, enthusiastic, ambitious, and self-motivated. I am a highly-energetic-get-it-done team player that lives in the moment—whether hard at work or play, making the most of every experience.

▲ I am a warm-hearted, caring, spiritual, complicated, restless, introspective being, with a wicked sense of humor—moved by intimate and connected relationships.

▲ I am a passionate, innovative, humorous adventurer who improves the world from outside the box!

▲ I am equipped, empowered, anointed, clear, direct, and full of vision, poised and positioned to help others and change lives by my ray-of-sunshine approach and ability to uplift those around me.

Can you see the beauty of each of these souls in their unique essences? Even as I write this, I smile, knowing and having experienced each of these individuals in a deeply personal way. I love the words they have chosen to reflect their own soul learnings—the discovery of their very essences.

My own essence statement sits prominently on my desk so that I can see it every day.

The Essence of Kami

*I am a passionate and wild soul with a thread
of quiet wisdom running through.
I love to dance in the energy of nature, people,
and the mysteries of life in great joy and happiness.*

Not only do I see it every day, but when things start to feel like they're out of whack—for instance, when things aren't going the way I want them to go—I can usually ground back into who I am and see that I'm not staying aligned to who I am and that I've somehow strayed off course.

You too will have a deeper knowing, after writing your Essence of You statement. In time, you will be ready to look for ways to gift your beautiful essence into the world. At this point you might be wondering what it is that you will do with this newfound awareness. Who will you share this gift with? How can it matter to those most important around you? These are the questions we will explore next.

Reflection

1. Share your Essence of You statement with a friend.
2. Consider these questions and journal on them. Don't judge. Just be curious and aware.
    - ▲ In what parts of your life are you fully living into your essence?
    - ▲ Are there some areas of your life where you might not be fully showing up as you?
    - ▲ Are there other areas of your life where you shine your essence brightly?

Embrace of Your Spirit Dreamer

The aqua glow of spirit pony shines amidst the deep forest bathed in golden light. She brings a reminder to look deep inside and honor your inner spirit.

Seek out conversations with your essence, not your circumstances. What are your dreams? What does your heart tell you? Life choices are yours alone, and your essence knows what to do. Soften your body. Soften your heart and receive the knowing gifts that come forth.

For it is your right to please yourself. It is your right to be happy and take charge. Embrace your very core, and your lovable heart and spirit will create their own inner glow that radiates unto the world. This is your life to live. Live it. Breathe it. Wear it. Most importantly, own it.

How Are You Meant to Matter?

"One is not born into the world to do
everything but to do something."
~ Henry David Thoreau

What is Your Purpose in This Lifetime?

Now is the time to make a commitment to your Self that there will be no playing small. For you have gifts to give unto the world—and a difference to make. Who are the real people around you that you can uplift, heal with a smile, or guide with your wisdom? How will you make a difference? What legacy do you want to leave in the world? How do you want people to remember you?

This is your purpose. This is how you're meant to matter. This is a big question that deserves deep contemplation, because being connected to your purpose and grounded in your most precious talents leads to an extraordinary life. This chapter is going to help you look deep into your soul to consider these important questions. I know from the work I do that understanding your purpose changes your life. I've seen it in my clients' lives, and I've experienced it in my own. You live in deeper meaning and you get up each morning knowing why you are here. There's a bigger internal driver that accelerates your growth and the opportunities that come into your life. This isn't the kind of driver that's based in crazy, busy long hours and relentless non-stop work. It's the kind of driver that is fire-driven through your heart and the Universe, collaborating in purpose together. There is a huge difference.

I believe that each and every one of us is meant to matter in our own unique way. Do you know how you're meant to matter? Your Essence of You statement has brought forth clarity with regard to your gifts, your talents, your passions, and all that you value. You were given these gifts for a purpose. You're now going to consider how you want your gifts to matter and will draft a Purpose Statement. This is a statement that is heart-driven— fueled by what inspires you, uplifted by what brings meaning to you. It expands upon who you are—the Essence of You—and moves into a declaration of how you can shine your essence out into the world.

So let's examine what a heart-driven Purpose Statement should do:

▲ Be written down.

▲ Focus on what you're MOST passionate about.

▲ Light you on fire.

▲ Be written in positive language.

▲ Be revised (when it doesn't light you on fire any longer or you have new passions to incorporate).

Review your Essence of You diagram. As you look across all of the fabulous words that paint the vision of who you are at your very essence, consider the following statements:

▲ I am at my best when …

▲ I really love to do …

▲ If I couldn't fail and had unlimited resources, I would…

Engaging your mind, body, and soul in your Purpose Statement is what sparks the deepest meaning in this exploration. Now think about and answer the following questions:

1. What gets my mind excited? What do I like to read? What do I find myself thinking about the most? What do I hope to learn about in the future?

2. How am I honoring my body (or how do I hope to in the future)? What does healthy living look like to me and how does that connect to my purpose, or does it? How would I change the way I live if I were to have a heart attack tomorrow?

3. What is my gut telling me right now about my purpose? What does my spirit tell me about the legacy I want to leave? How do I like to feed my soul?

Finally, consider the roles you serve in your life. Your roles might consist of mother, wife, friend, employee, boss, teacher, volunteer, coach, and even more. Think about the important people and what contributions you want to make.

- ▲ What are my roles?
- ▲ Who are the important people in my life?
- ▲ What contributions do I want to make in these roles?

These few short exercises give you fodder to work with—to ponder over—in order to create your unique Purpose Statement. There's no wrong or right way to do this. The goal is to keep it short and make it memorable.

What's important is that you make it yours—something that resonates with you. If you're a visual person, incorporate some fun and meaningful images that light you up. If you're an audial person, find a song that stands for your purpose and play it often. As you get the words right, and your statement lights you up when you say it out loud, you're on to something. Like your Essence of You statement, this exercise may take time. You may write the initial draft and need to let it simmer, then come back to it with a little added fuel to stoke the flames.

Okay, let's give this a try. Write this down in a three- to four-sentence statement—your Purpose Statement. Invite your light to shine out to others in all its glory. This is the final item to add to your Essence of You diagram. Once you feel it is complete, write your Purpose Statement below and add it to your Essence of You diagram. This is the foundation of why you're here on this earth in this lifetime. It is your purpose. It is your mission in life.

My Purpose Statement: _____

_____

_____

_____

_____

When I wrote my own Purpose Statement many years ago, I had the intention of returning to the corporate world. It was about a year after I'd been laid off in the biggest recession of my lifetime. Luckily, not many "vice president of marketing" jobs could be found at that time; otherwise, I would have jumped right back in and not continued my journey of discovery.

At the time I wrote my Purpose Statement, I knew I wanted to make a difference: "I want to improve the world, creating relationships and synergies by leading in a positive, passionate environment that is grounded in the oneness of our Universe."

Interestingly, I thought my tribe—the group who would receive my gifts—would be in a corporate setting. What I didn't understand at the time was that all exploration like this is really a journey. There's no such thing as a step-by-step course to living an extraordinary life. It's a journey that is always unfolding. The road twists and turns and is rarely a straight line. Experiences shape your journey. People who enter your life evolve your journey. Every day has something new to bring to your journey.

In that first year, I hadn't really discovered my tribe. While I'd gotten very clear about my essence, I hadn't found true clarity about how my gifts would matter in the world or for whom.

It starts by playing in the question. How do I want to matter? It will evolve—many times over the course of your lifetime.

I wish I could tell you there is a five-step process to discover your purpose. It's not that simple. This is a journey and each day dawns a new insight into how your gifts are meant to matter. Take this time to explore. Practice letting go of a need to control how or where things take you—particularly if you have been living a fast-paced, driven life. Remember, you are stepping into a new way of life—*being*.

Be gentle and patient with yourself, especially when it feels like nothing is moving—when it feels like forward movement has ceased and you're in the midst of a giant pause. Trust that in these pauses something is simmering. New ideas are shaping. Or perhaps new experiences are headed your way that will provide you with new ways of thinking or new ways of being. Be curious about who is showing up in your life. There are clues in the pauses. Clues to help you piece together what's next.

When I began to write this book, I initially did a Book-in-a-Weekend course where I vigorously put out 11,000 words. Afterwards, I read it and wasn't in love with the writing, but I didn't know where to take it. So, my book sat for a year—a year that generated huge growth for my business, which was essential for its sustainability. In that year new ideas evolved as well—my own learning expanded. I became more aware of the emotions that kept me playing small. I started to work with a coach who helped me recognize my own self-imposed boundaries of comfort. I didn't want to do public speaking. My networking was with people I already knew, because it was comfortable. One of the biggest self-imposed boundaries I regularly said out loud was, "I don't really need to make the kind of money I made in the corporate world, because I love what I am doing." Talk about filling my head full of limiting beliefs. I was definitely playing small.

This wonderful coach helped me see beyond these limiting beliefs. She looked at me one day and said, "You have huge gifts to give. Who are you to withhold these gifts? Get out there and deliver them in bigger ways ... to more people, with more expression ... own it!"

That statement forever changed my life. It was scary. I doubted my gifts. I put up roadblocks. Yet, I anxiously started to say yes to every opportunity that came my way. I put my own personal stake of conviction into the ground. "Yes, I can make the kind of money I made in my corporate days doing this work I love!" I acknowledged that the work I do makes a huge difference in people's lives and I need to share this gift. With each new scary step I took, my area of comfort grew.

One day in the midst of this expanding confidence, I picked up the phone and started to make calls to some of the most influential women I knew. I asked them to participate in a program called Extraordinary Women Connect. And they said yes. Those two months of wildly-driven vision created a new dimension to my business.

Ironically, during that year, I continued to coach women to step into playing in larger games—to play bigger than they'd done previously. Living through my own experiences and through those of my clients, I began to see some of the missing elements in my original 11,000-word manuscript. I had to go deeper.

I realized I had outgrown my original Purpose Statement that I'd written a few years earlier. So I took myself on a weekend retreat where I expanded how I wanted to matter in the world. My statement transformed into the following:

"My life journey is to uplift and empower women into their passions, so that they live into their full potential and leave a legacy that matters. I will be a person who has touched millions of women's lives around the world, helping them dance into lives full of passion and meaning. The ripple effect of my life's work—my teachings, my books, and my inspirational programs—will impact women everywhere. My daily mantras are: (1) Courage to live large; (2) Dream and play in soul-inspired thoughts and words; and (3) Determination thrives."

It was with these words that I began to see what needed to come to the surface in my writing and my work. This clarity fueled movement from the pause. But the pause had been an important part of the journey. It was from that pause that I found the meaning and significance in my purpose in order to make a deeper commitment to my work going forward.

And yes, this statement is big and bold. I recently had someone say to me, "Wow, a million women is a lot of women." Yes, that is true. But it fuels me to say yes to the opportunities that come my way—no matter how big or scary they may seem. It helps me step outside my comfort zone, when I otherwise might sit back and stay in what's familiar. Being willing to step out in such a big way makes my Purpose Statement powerful.

As you create your Purpose Statement, have fun in this part of your journey. Take yourself on a retreat where you can focus to gain clarity on how you're meant to matter. When you love the statement you create, share it with friends and family. Even more importantly, begin to share it with the people you want to help—those for whom you seek to make a difference. You're planting the seeds of something very important here.

Reflection

1. If you write your first draft of your Purpose Statement and you aren't in love with it, play in a bit of Steven Covey wisdom with his online personal mission statement builder. You've done a great deal of work to lead into this, so this exercise can help you hone in the words that are right for you. I used this when I wrote my last statement. The tool leads you to create a longer statement than you might like for your own Purpose Statement, but the exercise helped me identify some key components that I wanted to incorporate into my own. This free online tool is available at: http://www.franklincovey.com/msb/
2. At the end of each day, journal on my Extraordinary Life Mantra:
   ▲ Courage: How did I show courage today?
   ▲ Dream: What am I dreaming for my future?
   ▲ Determine: What am I determined to do tomorrow?

Renew

The lone horse stands powerfully in a glowing heart. It is time to renew your hope. Renew your faith. Renew your dreams. For all begins anew today.

Live each moment with purpose. If you know your purpose, re-commit to it. If your purpose remains elusive, ponder why you were put on this earth. What is in your heart that moves you? Listen. Embrace it. Vision it. Paint the picture in your mind. Write it into words. Breathe life into it.

11

Dreaming the Possibilities
of What Could Be

"Shoot for the moon. Even if you miss,
you'll land among the stars."
~ Les Brown

With your newfound awareness of who you are at your essence and your Purpose Statement, it's time to open the doors to dreaming. There are no limits to dreaming. There is no idea too wild and wacky—for it is here that innovation is found. It is here that we step outside the box of current reality to begin to see glimpses into the possibilities that can unfold for our lives.

Before going further, let's take a moment to explore a few of the great dreamers whose dreams became reality:

▲ When Martin Luther King, Jr. painted the vision of his dream, our nation was deep in the burrows of racial conflict. His "I Have a Dream" speech depicts vision spoken from the heart, filled with wild passion, deep-rooted values, and a belief that things could be different.

▲ Steve Jobs—a revolutionary dreamer of our times—declared his dream to "put a computer into the hands of everyday people" in 1976. In 2014, less than forty years later, 84% of American households had a computer and 40% of those households had more than one computer.

▲ When President John F. Kennedy, Jr. stood before the national television audience and declared, "We will go to the moon," there was no doubt that within the multitude of viewers a rumbling crowd of skeptics existed. But with those words of conviction he drew believers. The power of that statement led to man's first steps on the moon, opening a whole new frontier into the world of space.

Can you imagine if any one of these visionaries had placed themselves in a box of limited possibilities? If Dr. King had buried that dream inside his soul that so desperately had a calling? If Steve Jobs had set the dream of the personal computer on his garage shelf? If President Kennedy had modeled that speech to the nation in politically safe and cautious wording? So often this is what we do when we consider the dreams we hold for our lives. We listen to the naysayers around us or we let our own inner critic show up and tell us things like, "Don't be silly. That's not possible. That's not what you're supposed to do."

For years, I painted myself into that box. At one point, I thought to myself, *I'm a marketing executive who has always worked in the corporate world.* I could not see outside of the box I had painted for myself. I had mentors encourage me to start my own business, and I readily assured them that I wasn't an entrepreneur—I was a ladder-climbing corporate girl tried-and-true. What I hadn't yet discovered was that the essence of my gifts could and should matter and be used in a different way.

Dreaming can open up your heart to ideas you didn't even know existed for you. One of my clients, Barbara, spent an afternoon creating a vision board—a simple, yet very powerful, way to embark upon a dream journey. With a big empty poster board, a stack of magazines, a pair of scissors, and a glue stick, she made herself a pot of tea and lit some candles. As she browsed through the magazines looking for photos and words that inspired her, a photo of a beach cottage jumped out at her. It had a pretty front porch with white pickets and cozy chairs, just steps from the beach.

Barbara lived in the foothills of Colorado, and she was surprised that this picture called to her so intensely. She pasted the image right in the center of her poster board. When we later sat down together to talk about her finished board, she lit up vibrantly as she talked about the vision of this beach house, chuckling to herself, "I don't even know why this calls to me so much. I don't have any intention of moving to the ocean."

Six months later, through a series of fortuitous events, I got a very special phone call from her. She was walking her Great Pyrenees on the beach in Cape Cod, just steps away from the beach cottage she had rented for a year. She was whirling in the wind, dancing and laughing, saying, "Thank you! Thank you! Thank you!"

Now is the time for you to consider your gifts in this way—outside the limitations of any boxes—fully tuned into your heart, your essence, and how you can matter to the world. If you make anything happen in your world and in your life, what would it look like? Dream about different roles. Don't turn any idea down. Paint the picture of what you'd like to have in your world, your realm, on a day-to-day basis.

Powerful dreaming is an evolutionary process and, yes, a journey. I don't believe that a single exercise can open the door to the biggest dreams. It most likely will take a series of exercises and experiences to make that happen. So, begin to open the door to your dreams with any one of the following exercises. Then, go back and do another. There is great power in dreaming—so do as many as you wish, or even all of them! You might even repeat them whenever your heart is calling for a bit of dreaming. For example, I do a vision board every year. It keeps ideas flowing and gives me space to dream of what can be. I grow. Even more important are those times when I look back at my vision board and realize the link to what I've accomplished from my prior year's vision. Yes, there is great power in dreaming. So dream!

In Carmine Gallo's book, *The Innovative Secrets of Steve Jobs*, Gallo tells the story of a Disney executive charged with revitalizing the Disney stores. The executive turned to Steve Jobs—one of their largest shareholders—for advice. Jobs told the executive, "Go *bigger*." And that's what I say to you: "Go Bigger!"

Reflection

A Dream Walk through Nature to Envision Your Future

Set out on a walk on your favorite path and allow yourself to imagine yourself five years from now, at a time when you are living a life aligned to the core Essence of You. Who are you called to be? What are you excited about? What do you see around you? Who is around you? What do you notice about yourself when you dream of this future? Let the ideas dance! Carry your journal with you and when you feel inspired, sit down in all of nature's glory to write what has come forth—what is being revealed!

Dream Exploration Questions

▲ If you could have three wishes, what would they be?

▲ Thinking about the times you were most happy, what would you want to carry into the future?

▲ Looking into the future, who are you called to be? What work are you called to do?

▲ In twenty years, what is the one thing you will have wished you had done? What about in thirty years?

▲ What do you notice about yourself when you dream of the future?

▲ If you could communicate with yourself in the future, what questions would you want to ask yourself? What would you like others to ask of you?

▲ What would your mentor wish for you in the future?

Vision Board

Spend an afternoon with a stack of magazines, a poster board, a pair of scissors, and a stick of glue. Make yourself a nice pot of tea and just start thumbing through the pages. Watch for photos that make your heart leap. Notice the words that jump off the page at you. Quiet your busy mind and don't try to figure out the meaning of what you're drawn to—just allow whatever inspires and excites you to come forth. Clip away and watch the vision of your future unfold.

Possibilities Book

Start out with a shopping trip for a beautiful journal that calls out to you from the shelf. When you get it home, create dividers that depict different pieces of your life. For example, include Family, Friends, Career, Fun, Romance, Health, Finance, and Home. Make the categories relevant to your unique journey and be sure to include areas of passion or values that are important. Take care to make these page dividers beautiful and artistic. Then, similar to creating a Vision Board, set aside an afternoon of clipping, gathering, and dreaming—and fill your Possibility Book pages with visions of all that can be in your life.

Write a Story About Your Ideal Day

How does it start? What do you have time to do as your day progresses? What activities, people, and events inspire you throughout your ideal day?

Write a Letter of Celebration

Imagine it is one year from now and you are writing a letter to someone you deeply care about who would want to celebrate your success. Write about what you have accomplished during the past year … as if it has already happened. Connect with your heart and how you want to feel one year from now. Write what comes to mind when you are in that feeling place. Balance what you would love to have happen in your life with what you believe can happen.

Speeches of Passion

Watch Martin Luther King, Jr.'s "I Have a Dream," John F. Kennedy, Jr.'s "We will go to the moon," and Steve Jobs' "Stanford Commencement" speeches on YouTube. As you watch these powerful videos, note how King, Kennedy, and Jobs show their passion and paint the vision of the future. They are master teachers in understanding the expression of passion.

Free

"All good things are wild, and free." ~Henry David Thoreau

Like the wind in the trees, like a herd of wild horses in the rolling hills, honor your freedom today. Let the colors radiate from your soul and shine on all of those around you.

In the realm of freedom, your heart leads the way. The natural pull toward one direction or another lives within you. You need not ponder in your mind – you only need to feel where your heart wants you to go. Your direction may not be straight. It may meander along many trajectories. Know that this is as it should be.

12

Designing a
Dream-Inspired Life

"Success isn't a result of spontaneous combustion.
You must set yourself on fire."
~ Arnold Glasow

The dream phase of your journey casts a wide net. It opens your window to glimpses of possibilities you didn't even know existed and perhaps some that have been deeply seated in the knowing of your heart for years.

It's now time to begin to filter through the many possibilities that exist and focus in on the ones that call to you the most. Which ones light you up with a jolt of excitement? Are you amping up your impact in work you're already doing and in love with? Are you manifesting new people into your life—new relationships? Could your gifts be applied to an entirely new field or industry—perhaps an area you haven't even thought about yet? Are there any ideas you've been dreaming about for years but have kept on the backburner? Or maybe you convinced yourself they simply weren't possible. Exploring questions like these fuel your inspiration and dawn new ideas. It takes you deeper into your journey of possibility and gives you a framework from which to start making choices.

One of my clients, Rita, a technical leader in a fast-moving high-tech company, originally came to work with me as her coach, to focus on growing as a leader. She was seeking that next promotion, which she landed in the first year we worked together.

Ah, but there was still something more calling to her. Rita had grown up in India and watched her dad practice meditation for as long as she could remember. In her crazy-busy workplace, she incorporated mindfulness practices regularly, which helped her stay grounded in her own inner peace. They also created a peaceful environment for those around her. Her teammates often came to her office, quietly shutting the door behind them, to seek solace and guidance in the busy-ness of their work environment. She started to acknowledge her gift for bringing peace to others and wondered if she could build a career path that intentionally created peaceful space for others.

Rita had worked hard to get to this point in her career, so she deliberated if she could just walk away from it. As she explored this question, she wrestled with the choices before her. Rita began to formulate ideas—visions of meditation spaces in nature and leading leadership retreats to India. She did her homework.

She went to conferences about mindfulness. With time and focused intention, she began to connect the dots that would paint and give shape to the vision of her future. She knew in her heart that she had found the pathway for herself. One day, fully equipped with her research and her dreams, she quit that corporate job and stepped into the world of mindful leadership, as she launched her own company.

When I asked Rita how she knew the time was right, she replied, "Something unidentifiable began bubbling vigorously inside. I knew I needed to do work that was meaningful. And everything about my work environment screamed that it was time for change. I went through multiple bouts of flu because my immune system was so weak. Something had to shift. But mostly, I intuitively knew it was time. I knew that this was the right choice. I simply knew. I let go of the fear and moved forward."

Another one of my clients, Susan, had a great job in the energy industry, but had begun to have thoughts about starting her own consulting company. In her exploration process, she began to speak with people in her industry, and as a result, two different companies began to court her expertise, inviting her to join their firms.

While she was still undecided about which direction she would take, she needed to tell her existing company that she was leaving—there was a key project that she was being asked to lead, which she knew she wouldn't see through to the end. Upon telling her boss that she was leaving, the president of the company reached out to her to see what they could do to get her to stay, telling her, "Define the job you'd like to have here."

Suddenly, Susan had multiple job offers. She also still had budding thoughts of starting her own company. Together, we looked at these options in depth, evaluating the pros and cons. We took time to compare the roles against her essence, and particularly, her values. She considered the work that moved her the most and balanced that against how she would be spending her time in the various choices. In the end, Susan decided to take one of the offers from a new company, because she would be able to spend more of her time doing what she loved most. Today, she is a national spokesperson for her industry, sharing her expertise, and is often featured on national news.

When I asked Susan how our work together helped her make that decision, she shared, "It provided me with a decision framework to weigh my choices and to confidently step into my "what's next." This work enabled me to articulate what I was looking for in a new role. It made a big difference throughout the interview cycle, as I could clearly communicate my value and was able to define exactly what I was looking for. I know I made the right decision in my career move because of all the careful thought and reflection I had done."

So now it's your turn. Right now, without applying any limiting filters, tune into your heart and see what is most interesting to you. Set aside the "hows," the "yeah-buts," and any thoughts that pull you away from just considering the possibilities.

From a work perspective, if you are having a hard time choosing between different career paths, consider each option in light of your Essence of You diagram. It's particularly useful to consider your values against each option. For example, if having free time is one of the top values that you've identified for yourself, do any of your options provide stronger time freedom and flexibility? If creative expression ranks high, consider which pathways might fulfill you most in that arena. Pick your top ideas and begin to have conversations with people who are doing the kinds of things you dream about. Be curious. If it's an entirely new field of interest you are exploring, what can you learn about the field? Who is doing work there that is interesting? You'll be amazed at how readily people who have a passion for their work love to share about their industry.

If it's a lifestyle you want to design, look for role models to speak with who are living the way you envision. Who has made the kinds of changes in their life that inspire you? Ask them how they made the transition? Who helped them through that transition? If you want to take a trip around the world, find someone who has done that. Ask them about their experience. Ask them how they overcame roadblocks that might have been in their way. Ask them for advice.

It's all about exploration. Be curious. Ask questions. Look for others who are doing what inspires you. This exploration will no doubt spark new ideas for you, which will ignite a flame and take you further along in your discovery of what's next for you.

These conversations are essential fuel for understanding how others have successfully made changes in their lives. Listen to how they overcame obstacles that might have swayed their path. There is a good chance that these curiosity-inspired conversations will bring clarity in your heart—and help you see the pathway you're meant to travel. This is a journey of discovery. You're learning to listen to the light in others' hearts. You're recognizing the spark in your own heart. You're finding clarity. You are growing—personally, spiritually, and professionally.

Making Declarations

As your dream becomes clear—and a vision of what is possible is painted—it's time to go bigger and bolder! It's time to declare your intent. You're making a commitment to this dream and there's no turning back!

Let's look at what makes a great declaration. A declaration comes from the heart and is rooted in the passions that gave way to this idea. Remember, you've tuned into all that's meaningful in your world. You've woven the threads of your strengths and values into this dream. This dream is yours and yours alone.

Commit to this dream through a declaration. You will create what you declare! A good declaration is written in the positive, as if it's happening today. A good way to start your declaration is "I am doing …" or "I am …" It should be short and memorable—and rich with feeling and emotion. Something you can shout to the world. Something you can embody in every cell of your being. Paint the vision with your declaration.

Your declaration could be a theme that you own for a year, for example, "This is the year of owning my voice, and I'm going to do a TedTalk!" Or it can reflect a transformational journey in your life: "I am an author with a bestselling book!" or "I'm leaving my job this year to launch a successful business as a [coach, trainer, consultant]. Perhaps it's a role you aspire to: "I am the CEO of a company!" Or maybe your declaration is all about taking your life back: "I come first in my life!" Whatever your declaration, you have to feel a big resounding "YES" in your body when you claim it.

My Declaration Statement: _____

_____

_____

_____

_____

Strengthening Your Beliefs –
The Power of Positive Thought

Sometimes when you make a big and bold declaration like this, the little voice in the back of your head shows up and says, "Who do you think you are to make such a claim?" "That's a ridiculous and impossible idea!" or "That's a grand idea, but you don't have the [money, people, resources] to bring this into reality."

Stop there! Don't let this go any further. Instead, I want you to visualize what can be. Visualize it every day.

When Walt Disney was on his death bed, a trusted friend sat next to him expressing his sorrow that Walt would not get to see the Epcot Center come to fruition. Walt patted the friend's hand and reassured him, "I know exactly what the Epcot Center is going to look like ... I've envisioned it every day for the past fifteen years."

That is the power of visualization and Walt lived it in his life every day. Visualize your dream every day.

Did you know we have on average 60,000 thoughts a day? And the scary thing is that 95% of those thoughts are the same as the ones we had yesterday. I'm going to invite you to shake it up. Your journey is directly related to these thoughts. If you play a tape of limiting beliefs through your mind all day long, you will get exactly that—limited success. If you play a tape of empowering beliefs in your mind all day, you will be empowered and successful in anything you do.

So, let's look at the beliefs you hold about your declaration. Do you believe at your very core that you can accomplish this declaration? Let's go deeper!

First, make a list of all the empowering beliefs you have about your declaration that are power-charged. For example, you may say, "I'm really good at ____. I am creative, I make things happen, I am passionate about ____, I have great experience doing ____."

1. _____

_____

2. _____

_____

3. _____

_____

4. _____

_____

5. _____

_____

6. _____

_____

7. _____

_____

8. _____

_____

9. _____

_____

10. _____

_____

Consider how these beliefs strengthen your declaration, and how they empower you to succeed. These are the types of thoughts that will uplift you and keep you moving—even when times get bumpy. Things do get bumpy when you're making big life changes. The conviction in empowering beliefs will carry you over those mountaintops and through the most challenging moments.

Now, I want you to list the beliefs that put limits on your declaration. These limiting beliefs take the wind out of your sails, drown the ideas that want to flourish, and stamp out the fire of your passion. They don't empower you. Examples might be, "I'm not good enough," or "There isn't enough ____." Dig deep—I can almost guarantee that you have some limiting beliefs.

1. _____

_____

2. _____

_____

3. _____

_____

4. _____

_____

5. _____

_____

6. _____

_____

7. _____

_____

8. _____

_____

9. _____

_____

10._____

_____

Compare how you felt as you wrote these two lists. Did you notice a difference in your body? Did the vision of your declaration brighten or fade as you wrote each list? Did you feel any pain associated with each limiting belief? What do you believe are the consequences when you spend those 60,000 thoughts each day on limiting beliefs? If you said they will cost you your dream, you're right! But the good news is that you get to decide the types of beliefs you breathe into your life each day. You have a choice.

Let's look back at those limiting beliefs and explore what it might take to transform them into empowering beliefs. For each limiting belief, write a new empowering belief, striking through that initial statement you wrote.

For example, there was a time when I told myself, "You're not good at public speaking." I rewrote this belief a few years back as follows. "When I speak I inspire people to action in their lives. I create change. I touch people's hearts." Today when I speak I do these things. I can move a room. This is empowering.

Another limiting belief could be: "I don't have enough money to pursue this dream." You could rewrite this declaration with: "I have an abundant flow of resources and unlimited possibilities to create this dream. My mind is open to see creative ways to manifest this dream."

You are addressing the elephant in the room by acknowledging these limiting beliefs. When you rewrite them and convert them to empowering beliefs, you quiet these noisy voices in the back of your mind and give them new focus.

Owning Your Declaration

When you have removed all of the limiting beliefs from your language and practice envisioning your success every day, supported with empowering beliefs, you will feel the momentum shift. Suddenly, new people will come into your life and opportunities will drop into your lap. It's truly magical. This is the time to be uber-aware of shifts and changes all around you. This is the time to be on hyper-alert for signposts. Those shifts, changes, and signposts represent the impact of manifestation starting to take shape in your life.

Share your declaration with your champions who support your vision. Practice owning the vision and painting the pictures to all who will listen. Take a hike into the wilderness, climb atop a rock, and shout to the world your intentions. Declare, declare, declare!

When I was in an important part of my own journey of transformation, I was lucky enough to be on the northern coast of California. This coastline sings to my soul in a deep and empowering way. As the powerful waves pulled away from a large rock jetting from the sea, I scrambled to the top, breathing in the salty cold spray. I lifted my arms to the sky and shouted my intentions to the world knowing I would never look back. That vision continues to empower me every day.

This is what I wish for you. That feeling of empowerment will carry you through the rocky moments. More importantly, that feeling of empowerment will carry you into your celebration of success.

Our Deepest Fear
- Marianne Williamson, *A Return to Love*

Our deepest fear is not that we are inadequate.
Our deepest fear is that we are powerful beyond measure.
It is our light, not our darkness that most frightens us.
We ask ourselves, Who am I to be brilliant,
gorgeous, talented, fabulous?
Actually, who are you not to be?
You are a child of God.
Your playing small does not serve the world.
There is nothing enlightened about shrinking so that
other people won't feel insecure around you.
We are all meant to shine, as children do.
We were born to manifest
the glory of God that is within us.
It's not just in some of us; it's in everyone.
And as we let our own light shine,
we unconsciously give other people
permission to do the same.
As we are liberated from our own fear,
our presence automatically liberates others.

Reflection

Take your declaration out in nature. Climb atop a mountain, a rocky shoreline, or even a boulder. Shout your declaration out to the world.

Become accustomed to telling people about your declaration. If your declaration is about becoming an artist, introduce yourself as an artist. If you write regularly, introduce yourself as an author. If your dream is to be an entrepreneur, own the gift you wish to give to the world in that work. For instance, "I am a healer," "I help people live a mindful life," "I change corporate cultures." Be aware of how you embody this declaration and verbalize it from your inner core—your power center. Imagine the statement energetically flowing out into the world. The more you say it out loud, declare it—and embody it—the more real it becomes to others and, more importantly, to you.

Follow Your Star

Shining brightly above you, a star aligns brightly to your path and purpose. If you take in the wholeness of the twinkling lights against the dark backdrop, that single star will, in right time, present itself to you as yours.

Sit in quiet peacefulness until the glowing brilliance of that one star – your star – calls to you. Ponder the question why it has chosen you. Is it perhaps its location? Is it perhaps its color or its brilliance? Or perhaps it just has a special message to deliver, that is only yours. Just live in the question and see what comes forth.

Know this star is there for you to turn to for guidance and growth. It knows of your path and purpose and can help you connect and reconnect as often as need be. For it is your star.

13

The Action of Success

*"Vision without action is merely a dream.
Action without vision just passes the time.
Vision with action can change the world."
~ Joel A. Barker*

With your vision and declaration firmly in place, it's time to set your sails in motion. It's time to set your goals and step into action. This is the "how" that I previously told you to put on the back burner. It's time to plan and build a process of accountability to keep you moving.

As I found my clarity in my own purpose in life, the task-doer in me diligently jumped into the flurry of being an entrepreneur, wearing dozens of hats that at one time in my career had been supported by a staff of many. I was the strategist, the marketer, the implementer, the sales person, the IT director, the assistant, the CEO, the coach—to name just a few. As a leader in the corporate world, I had a great deal of productivity and project management experience and had always prided myself in being someone with a reputation for getting things done—I was an action taker, a multi-tasker, a conductor of many.

Yet, in this new state of complexity as entrepreneur, I was struggling with the many balls I had in the air. There were so many actions I was solely responsible for that my days quickly became a roadmap of interruptions and knee-jerk redirections.

A friend of mine invited me to attend a Franklin Covey "7 Habits of Highly Effective People" class she was teaching, and I accepted the invite, mostly because I wanted to see her in action as a teacher. At the time, I didn't feel that I really needed help with how to be more effective. I had taken the course years before. Although I didn't remember all of the specifics, I figured I had all those principles down. After all, I had been quite successful as the one who got things done.

I chuckle at this self-perception now, because those two days in that "7 Habits" class grounded a set of practices in my work that would help reshape how I ran my small company. The bottom line is that good planning and intentional action is not an elementary skillset. It is a set of skills we have to diligently practice and evolve. Planning and intentional action is a skillset we will have to practice and re-master for the rest of our lives.

The reintroduction to these principles led me down a path to becoming a student focused on the art of goal setting and prioritization. Even today, when I teach my clients principles for how to step into action and stay focused, I continually remind myself to stay in practice myself. Just like everyone else, it's easy to get distracted or waylaid in the balance of the many things that go on in my life each day, each week, each month, each year.

So I invite you to delve into this chapter with care—and not to brush it off as something you already know. Yes, you have gotten to the place you are in your life because you have engaged in planning and action focus. But I assure you, the mere refocus on this intent will fine tune your mastery.

Goal Setting

People approach goals in all sorts of ways. Some people avoid them altogether; others think about them but never write them down; while others are diligent about goal writing. I believe in writing down your goals.

There's a wonderful study that was done with a Harvard Business School graduating class. At graduation, they found that eighty-four percent of the class had no goals. Thirteen percent of the classmates had goals but hadn't written them down. Only three percent of the class had written goals. What's fascinating is taking a look at the earnings of these graduates ten years later. The thirteen percent who had goals but hadn't written them down were earning on average twice as much as those without goals. However, the three percent who had written goals were earning on average ten times as much as the other ninety-seven percent of the graduates.

This study highlights the importance of goals. I like to take goal-setting and goal-writing one step further. I like goals to be provocative—to be a real stretch. Again, I'm going to take you back to Steve Job's challenge—"Go Bigger!"

Here are the components of provocative goals:

1. Bold and Far Reaching
   "Shoot for the moon. Even if you miss, you'll land among the stars." ~Les Brown

2. Heartfelt
   "Success isn't a result of spontaneous combustion. You must set yourself on fire." ~Arnold H. Glasow

3. Unconditionally Positive
   "The positive thinker sees the invisible, feels the intangible, and achieves the impossible." ~Unknown

4. Written as if It's Happening Today
   "If you change the way you look at things, the things you look at change." ~Dr. Wayne Dyer

5. Written with a Deadline in Mind
   "Goals are dreams with deadlines."
   ~Diana Scharf Hunt

For example, if you want to focus on your health this year, a good goal might sound like: "I am living a healthy life, where I exercise regularly, get enough sleep, put nourishing food into my body, and maintain optimal weight so that I look fabulous, feel fantastic, and have tons of energy. By the end of this year, I will beat my personal best when I run a half-marathon."

Another important thing about goals is that they should span all the important parts of your life. Go back to your values and consider what really matters to you. Add in goals around your passions and what lights you up with excitement. Perhaps you will set goals for spiritual growth, your health, or working in your art. Maybe you want to write a children's book, or there might be a new relationship you want to manifest in your life. Perhaps you want to strive for that promotion or find a new job. Or maybe this is the year you want to start your own business. You get to choose!

I've included space for five goals—you may have three; you may have six. It is your choice. Be realistic about how much change you can take on in one year. It's better to put your focus on a few high-impact goals than to spread yourself too thin in many.

Connect back to your declaration and decide which goals will help you make that declaration a reality. Which goals will bring the most happiness and joy to your life? Which ones will light your world on fire? Once you've identified them, write down your goals for this year.

My Provocative Goals:

1. _____

_____

_____

_____

2. _____

_____

_____

_____

_____

3. _____

_____

_____

_____

4. _____

_____

_____

_____

5. _____

_____

_____

_____

Circle the number one goal you want to accomplish in the next year. This will be your *keystone goal*, which will help you prioritize your actions later. It will help you make the tough choices you need to make when you consider your time and resources. Your keystone goal should be visible every day. Find an inspirational quote that represents this goal—and hang it on your bathroom mirror so you see it every day. Or find something in nature that reflects the essence of your goal, and keep it on your desk so you can actually touch and feel the importance of this goal. Your keystone goal should be a guiding light in your year—helping you make choices and stay focused, and guiding your intentions on a daily basis.

Sometimes your goals may actually appear to be in opposition to each other. For example, one of your goals might be to travel the world, while another might be to open a storefront business. I encourage you to look beneath the surface of this potential conflict. Perhaps there are ways to combine those aspirations. For example, could you open a storefront business and import items for your store while you travel? Stay open to synchronicities that might occur.

If you find, however, that there truly is a conflict or you feel as if you're taking on too much all at once, be realistic. It's okay to cross off one or two goals for now, keeping only the ones that make your heart sing. This lets you focus on the ones that matter most. You are the driver of your own destiny here. Be realistic. But be brave and courageous too.

Stepping into Action

Goals are beautiful and powerful. But goals without action will remain just lovely words posted on the wall. So let's start with something simple. What's one action you can take today—right now in this moment—that will start the wheels of motion toward your goals? Ponder this for a moment. What are the steps you will need to make in order to get to that end result? Once you've identified that first action step, put this book down and get up and do it. There is nothing more uplifting to your journey than taking action!

Record what you did here: _____

_____

_____

_____

_____

Now, let's get back to more action planning! For each goal you have set, take the following steps:

1. Paint the picture in your mind's eye of you successfully achieving that goal. How do you feel? What emotions uplift you when you've accomplished this goal? Describe the flow of what is happening around you and how it is impacting others. What are the accomplishments, the wins, the successes? Describe how your essence shines bright in the assured accomplishments that result from this goal.

   Now begin to define the steps you will take to make this happen. Is there new knowledge you must gain? What resources do you need? Define the steps you will take to bring this goal alive in your life within:

   a.   1 Day

   _____

   _____

   b.   1 Week

   _____

   _____

   _____

c.   1 Month

_____

_____

_____

d.   3 Months

_____

_____

_____

e.   6 Months

_____

_____

_____

f.   1 Year

_____

_____

_____

2. Now imagine you have a magic wand and can have
    three wishes granted to heighten the health and vitality
    of this goal. What would they be? What could you do
    to manifest these wishes in the action timeline you've
    just developed above? Add ideas that come to mind to
    your action plan.

3. Finally, I want you to dream into this goal one more
    time. Imagine it is three years from now. How has your
    life changed? Describe what you've manifested. What
    recognition and rewards have come your way as a
    result of your hard work and diligent follow-through
    toward this goal? How do you feel every day because
    you've accomplished this? How do you celebrate? Paint

the picture in any form you want! Write it, draw it, find something to represent this goal, and put it in a place where you can touch it and feel it. You could paint some rocks, draw a picture, journal about it, cut out an inspirational photo—anything that gives you a touch-point to come back to on a regular basis.

Putting Your Plan into Practical Action

When you have finished that big list of action items, chances are the whole list of to-dos might appear a little overwhelming. After all, there's a lot to get done. To start with, stop where you are. Take a big breath that goes deep—to your very core—to your very essence! Tune into that power of *you* that you know is there. Now, let's look at how you can weave a plan of action into your world.

> "The key is not to prioritize what's on your schedule, but to schedule your priorities." ~ Stephen Covey

The godfather of mastering planning, Stephen Covey, teaches us to put first things first, and make sure that we reserve time for the priorities that matter most. You've identified your goals as what matters most to you. Building a planning system into your life that will honor these goals is a critical and final step in your journey to achieve a life of passion, purpose, and meaning.

Here are some of my favorite tips to help you stay on track with your goals and the actions that will lead you to your success:

1. Keep your goals front and center always. Hang them in a prominent place where you can see them each day. Reconnect to them each week prior to planning your schedule.

2. Find a time to do your weekly scheduling, whether that's a Friday afternoon or Sunday night for the following week, or even first thing on Monday morning. Whatever day and time you choose, do it diligently.

3. Choose a calendar method—whether you go with a handwritten planner or an electronic Outlook approach—and schedule time for the things that are most important to you. Schedule time for exercise, family, important work projects—anything that has made it onto your goal list is important enough to schedule time to focus on.

4. Schedule time to think and time to strategize about your goals—especially your keystone goal. Set up a block of time every week where you turn off email, phones, and the potential for any interruptions so you can focus only on your big goals. I can't stress this enough. Evaluate how you are doing on your actions. Consider if there are things you could be doing to fast track your progress. This practice will help to keep your goals at the forefront of your mind, so that they don't get lost in the hustle bustle of your life.

5. Keep a "To Do" list along with your calendar. I

leverage the *tasks* function of Outlook and keep a handwritten list to review with my accountability partner each week. This dual function seems to help me keep in check and on track. Again, just do it in a way that works for you.

6. Review your "To Do" lists and consider what's important for you to move forward in your journey. What's not important? Eliminate or minimize the things that aren't important. Just as your values can change over the course of your life, those tasks and action steps, and even your goals, need to be reviewed and adjusted as you continue along your journey. Through the lessons we learn along the way, or the clarity we gain, our priorities and actions can change

7. And speaking of accountability partners ... get one! There's nothing more powerful than a weekly meeting to share your progress. On weeks when things didn't go as you planned, your accountability partner can help you get back on track. They get to know your journey and can become a strategic partner in your success. And when the wins come, they can cheer you on.

8. Celebrate your successes! Share the little moments as well as the big ones. They create a surge of momentum that will unfold to bring more.

The Art of Balance – It's all Life After All!

I hear a lot of conversation about work-life balance. Perhaps it is time that we start thinking about work-life balance in a different way. After all, it's all life! For me, I prefer to use the term *work-life blending*. How do you intertwine passions, responsibilities, and personal joy amidst all these things that need to happen? The answer to this will be different for every person. And the blending equation will change as life progresses—it will never remain static or the same at all times in our lives.

The good news is that work-life blending starts with much of the work you've already done in this book. When you know who you are at your very essence and listen to the callings that come from that knowing, you can create an environment that lets your soul shine and your heart take flight. Here are some key principles to keep in mind:

- ▲ Have a passion in the work you do. Understand what moves you. Take time for the things that you value most: date nights, your children, faith, spirituality, and more.
- ▲ Be present wherever you are. When you're home with family, be present. When you're deep in your work, be present with it.
- ▲ The ability to multitask is a myth. There is solid research that tells us we are less productive when our minds are bouncing back and forth between projects. Focus on one thing at a time. Bucket your time for specific roles and responsibilities. For example, I see clients on Mondays and Wednesdays. When I get up on those days, I

know what my day will be about. Tuesdays are my CEO days—the days where I focus on my business growth. Fridays are my writing days. My weekends are for family and personal time and rarely involve work. Take time to figure out what your buckets are and start to schedule them into your calendar each week.

▲ Ask for help when you need it! Partner with others at home and at work.

▲ Develop a sense of community. This can be in your work or social environments, your volunteer efforts, or just the people you love most. Find shared interests with others and create a support system where you support one another.

▲ Learn to say no! Get rid of the things in your life that no longer serve you. Are there activities that energetically drain you? Are there people you no longer align with as you have grown? It's okay to say no.

While these principles provide a visual guiding light, your definition of balance will be unique to you. You've got unique priorities, values, and passions. If you connect deeply to these, you will discover new insights and approaches for how you can shift the balance equation in your life.

Reflection

Are you ready to explore your own work-life blending principles? Here's an exercise in the art of creating balance in your world. Find a friend to do this with, or just take some quiet contemplative time to explore on your own.

1. Recall a time in your life when you felt a sense of equilibrium—a time when you felt alignment to those around you: your family, your work, and most importantly, yourself; a time when you felt healthy, vibrant, mentally stimulated, and on fire with a strong sense of purpose. Tell a friend or write the story about this time in your life. What were you doing? Who was involved? What contributed to this sense of balance?

2. As you tell the story, look into the situation a little more deeply.

   ▲ How did your passions and values align to the world around you? What was it about you that contributed to the successful balancing act you created at this time—what personal strengths and gifts did you tap into?

   ▲ How were you making a difference in the lives of others? How were others making a difference in your life? What partnerships, be it with your work, your family, or your friends, made this time effective?

   ▲ How were you taking care of YOU at this time? How did you feel? Consider your whole Self—mind, body, emotion, spirit. What were the self-care factors that contributed to this sense of balance?

3. After you've explored your own stories, consider what principles were key to creating balance for your life. What could you shift today? What one small step could you take to put yourself on a path of balance?

4. How does this apply to the action plan you've created? What might need to shift or change? Make the changes in your plan.

Action with Impact

What's the one action you can take today that will make the difference you want to make tomorrow? Every day there are so many choices in how you spend your time. Today is about action – and it's about taking the best action with the most impact.

Consider how you can make a difference – perhaps it's in finding peace of mind in your own world or perhaps it's about creating abundance. It can be in your life or in the lives of others. The choice is yours. You are the catalyst to bring about change merely by combining the power of focused intention and focused action.

So consider your choices today and select your actions intentionally – then spring lightly into the world and create!

14

Emotions, Roadblocks and Obstacles

"Life isn't about waiting for the storms to pass.
It's about learning how to dance in the rain."
~ Vivian Greene

I wish I could tell you the road from here to where you're going is straight and without obstacles. That is not the truth. In fact, I can promise you that it will wind through valleys, over mountains, and even arrive at places you think are impassable. As you traverse this winding road, expect the unexpected.

The journey to greatness is just that way. Your commitment to your declaration will be tested and even reshaped. It won't look exactly the way you planned. It will evolve. Determine your true north and realize that there are many paths that can take you there. In fact, the road you find yourself on will be exactly the one you are supposed to be on. The experiences you encounter—whether positive, negative, or emotionally charged—will shape your spiraling growth. Those very experiences will continue to shape who you are and will be an intricate part of discovering the future gifts you will share with the world.

I believe in the power of positive thinking. I have studied the world of positive empowerment for many years. The journey you have come through up to this point has been all about shining a light on your positive strengths and recalling the positive experiences in your life. It's a powerful foundation.

What I also had to learn was how to embrace the bumpy segments in my journey—the parts that at first glance could be perceived as negative experiences. Even as I look back now at my own evolution, I chuckle at the places where I wanted to deny fear, sadness, or anger, the times when I wanted to ignore the emotions that didn't fit the positivity standard I had set for myself. Yet, I couldn't escape those moments, and the more I pushed them down and silenced their raucous calls, the more they slowed my forward momentum.

When I first launched my company, I was amazed at how quickly doors of possibility opened in those early days of my newfound clarity. Even on the very day I started my equine guided coaching training—a month-long intensive program at a ranch in Northern California—I received a synchronous gift to confirm that I was on the right journey. This gift helped me realize I was moving toward my purpose. The Universe delivered this gift in perfect timing.

On the Friday before I started my course, I got a call from a perfect prospect, saying he was interested in my coaching. We scheduled a time to talk by phone on the following Monday morning—the day I was scheduled to start my course—so that I could have the weekend to diligently plan for this first "sales" call. I awoke early on that Monday morning to allow plenty of time to set the intention for the call. In a shared houseful of other training participants, I shut the door and took that call sitting on the edge of my bed. At the end of that magical phone conversation, I had my first paying client!

Shortly after that event, I landed a great combo *consulting+coaching* gig and the money flowed to me effortlessly. It was like that during my entire first year—things came to me easily. The Universe provided.

Of course, starting a business and becoming an entrepreneur, after all my years of being a corporate girl, wasn't an entirely easy and smooth journey. I had more growth opportunities to encounter. There were more lessons for me to learn surrounding my purpose and my gifts. I had mountains I needed to climb—some really large ones. To traverse those mountains, the Universe delivered shifts and curves and turns along the way. The journey toward a deeper understanding of me as an entrepreneur and a coach came with emotions and worries.

In that first year, I refused to give voice to those fears and instead pushed them down and masked them in the positive events and circumstances that were taking place. The upbeat positive me took control. And, as a result, things began to get sticky. After a great first year, the flow of new possibilities slowed to a trickle, as did the income. What I didn't understand at the time was that most startup businesses go through ebb-and-flow cycles of growth and slowdown, expansion and contraction. It's a natural evolution. I didn't know this, but more importantly, I didn't want to feel the emotions that I attached to these unknown cycles.

One day in that second year, I visited my friend Lin's ranch for a day of mutual coaching with her herd of horses. It was a cold, yet sunny, spring day—with winds blowing sixty-mile-per-hour gusts. The ironic thing was that Lin was going to gift me an equine assisted coaching session with her and her horse Windy Day. Apparently, the wind had a message for me to learn that day.

As we started my coaching session, I was unclear what I wanted to focus on. You see, I was very practiced at only focusing on what was positive. I felt out of touch with what was stirring around inside of me and wasn't able to even put words to it. I took space in the round pen with Windy Day, and we both stood side-by-side, feet solidly planted in the ground. With our chests spread wide, we leaned into the wind that bit through my fleece jacket and pushed into the force of nature that wailed against us. After what seemed like a long time, Lin shared her observation of our stance and the way we leaned in and braced against the wind.

She then asked the question, "Does it feel like you're bracing against something in your life in this same way?" As I pondered her question, I recognized the feeling of this bracing in my life. I was determined I was going to make my entrepreneurial journey work. I was determined I wasn't going to ever go back to the corporate world. I was determined that my newfound purpose in life was right and it was on track. I was determined that I was going to make this venture work.

As Lin helped me uncover what lay beneath the bracing stance, she quietly asked me, "Is there fear under all this bracing?" Tears began to well up and my conflicting thoughts raced through my head. *No, I don't want fear to be a part of this journey. I need to stay in the positive!* But I could feel the fingers of fear stretching into every corner of my body. I turned to Lin and admitted, "Yes, I'm terrified. I'm terrified that this work that I love won't work out, that I won't be able to pay my bills, that I'll lose my beloved home, and that I won't know where my next client is coming from." We explored fear that day in all the dark corners where it existed. In bringing forth those fears and giving voice to them, a huge weight was lifted from my body.

After this session, I knew I needed to process my relationship with fear, and as I returned home that evening, I sat down and wrote a piece of inspiration. "Looking into the Eyes of Fear," would later become an intricate card in my daily inspirational card deck, *Pony Ponderings Inspiration Cards*.

As soon as I owned my fear, voiced it, and looked into the eye of my fears, all the inner stickiness I was feeling let loose. I learned a big life lesson that day: we can't ignore the emotions that come our way—no matter what they may be.

In the book, *Playing Big*, by author Tara Mohr, Tara shares that the bigger the idea—and the more it resonates with our own purpose—the bigger the fear we will experience. In other words, once you have found clarity in your purpose and you begin to step into the gifts you're meant to deliver in the world, fear will show up in big and pretentious ways.

Looking into the Eyes of Fear

Often, we have a tendency to set aside the emotion of fear, ignoring its presence and allowing it to wreak quiet havoc. Consider instead looking into the eyes of fear – and realizing it for what it is – an emotion. An emotion that brings meaning and message. It brings reason to explore deeper and consider in logic and in heart.

Today invite fear into the room. Intimately get to know the message it brings and realize that this sensation is normal – a part of your body's own journey and growth. Balance the energies of this emotion: from one side in the realm of positive possibilities and from the other side in the fullness of risk potential. Live in the flow between these sensations – play in the pivotal balance – adjusting weights, feeling your way through intuition and wisdom.

Then release yourself to the journey. Discover new life in new breath. Give this emotion permission to move through your body – perhaps settling temporarily into one spot or another – but in awareness you can breathe the emotion back into movement and action. No longer stuck in mass, but flowing in the movement that comes in acknowledgment. And with this movement comes the gift of growth.

The fear I was facing in that second year of my business was exactly that. I knew I had found my purpose in life. I knew I was making a huge difference in the lives of others. What I was doing resonated at my very soul level. That's why the fear was so enormous for me.

Mohr differentiates between two different types of fear: pachad and yirah, both terms derived from the Hebrew bible.

▲ Pachad is the fear of imagined possibilities that we make up in our mind. It's often over-reactive and originates from our reptilian brain that protected us from physical harm. In most circumstances, however, there isn't really a physical risk—it's merely the emotional risk we're responding to. It's the fight or flight mode that we find ourselves in when our emotions get triggered. Pachad tries to get us to avoid potential danger, without recognizing the possibilities of growth before us. We see only the most disastrous possibility that can be imagined … a worse-case scenario. We feel tightness and restriction in our bodies in response to pachad fear.

▲ Yirah is the type of fear we experience when we inhabit a larger space than we're used to and when we tap into our passions and move to expand our dreams. It provides a sense of more energy than we normally experience—a sense of awe. It's aligned to something sacred in our lives and comes from the soul. It often shows up when we're being vulnerable and courageous, honoring our perfect truth. In yirah, we are excited and uplifted in our body. While we manifest nervous energy in yirah, it's electrical and on fire. Yirah moves us, while pachad constricts us.

That day in the round pen with Windy Day, I uncovered a plethora of pachad fears. They were imaginary and made up in my mind. Despite the fact that I stood tall and strong in them, I was allowing the constricted energies of pachad to slow my progression. I doubted my capabilities and the possibilities before me. And perhaps most importantly, I had a lesson to learn about fear that would be essential to my own clients' future successes. That early slowdown of income and clients was critical in my own journey. I learned about fear—how to acknowledge fear, experience the emotion, and really feel it in my body. And I learned to trust in the abundance of the Universe, because as I made this shift, the energetic flow of abundant resources and people began to flow to me again. I had to experience the lessons of fear, for my own personal growth, but also so that I could skillfully guide my clients through their fears as they stepped into their biggest dreams and possibilities. It was another example of the Universe delivering exactly what I needed in my life.

Both of these types of fear are uncomfortable. Learning to recognize the type of fear you're experiencing will help you move through that fear more quickly with grace and understanding.

A few years ago, I decided to launch a series of events for wildly successful women, called Extraordinary Women Connect. I was surrounded every day by amazing women, and on any given day, I would find myself introducing one great woman to another great woman in an effort to create an explosion of new possibilities. I was in awe of the magic that resulted from these connections and the power of unfolding ideas that were launched.

It occurred to me that I had a gift for connecting people and wondered what would happen if I formalized a way to intentionally make more connections. Early on in the planning I was slowed by pachad fears. *Why would these senior high profile women say yes to participating? What if no one shows up? What if I take center stage and stumble upon my words? What if no one is inspired by what I've created?* I felt sticky as I attempted to move forward, and then sat on the idea for months.

As I examined each of these fears for what they were, I realized that there were not a lot of reasons to stop. I asked myself, "So what if this happens?" As a result, I began to realize that none of these fears were life threatening and the potential for success far exceeded the potential for failure.

I stepped into the fear. I made a list of women who I wanted to bring into the program—big names I loved that seemed outside my reach. And as I reached out to each one, and each enthusiastically said yes, I realized I was moving the vision. Yirah began to show up with a sense of excited energy—cheering me along to step into the realms of what could be. The explosion of new ideas and a sense of "unstoppability" swept over me. Again, I felt the sense of ease that unfolded, because I was on purpose and doing what I was supposed to be doing.

On the first Extraordinary Women Connect event I hosted, my yirah nerves energetically danced in my body. As I led that room that day, something inside me shifted … I relaxed into the energy. Suddenly, I felt a sense of awe for the women in the room and an appreciation for the gifts that each brought. There I stood amongst these crazy successful women, realizing that I'd earned the right to step into this space. This was yirah in full force. Yirah uplifts us into new possibilities and expands our world. It lights up the path before us to places and opportunities we would have missed otherwise. It helps us step into our soul's purpose.

I encourage you to embrace yirah with gentle care and appreciation for her affirmation of your purpose. Savor the jazzed emotion you feel and tune into it. Recognize that it's a gift and step into it fully—don't retract or withdraw from it! Dance in yirah's energy. Let it fill you with bright light and color. Yirah lifts you in your firedancer power with your own expansive wings supporting you. Live into it, dance into it, play into it. In this space, you are following your calling. Yirah is your biggest fan—your greatest supporter!

I can assure you that fear will be your traveling companion on your personal growth journey toward stepping into bigger platforms in your life. Your voice of doubt will show up and tell you that you're not good enough or smart enough. The opportunity before you is to examine these voices, allow them to be heard, and then embrace them with kindness and love.

So how do you manage these fears that will eventually show up? First of all, recognize which fear you're facing. I highly recommend reading Mohr's chapter on fear. In fact, it's become required reading for my clients when they're making big transformations in their lives. Fear can be a complex emotion. Acknowledging this, Mohr shares a whole toolbox for managing and responding to fear. What I particularly like is Mohr's awareness that we are each unique individuals, so she provides us with whole-body tools to meet fear head-on through our bodies, minds, and hearts.

Let's take a look at these three areas:

Body

Body-based tools mean doing something physically to or with our body to address fear. Go for a walk or a run, or, one of my favorites, do yoga. Practice slowing your breathing, taking deep intentional and focused breaths. Our bodies are amazing vehicles and a huge source of wisdom and ultimately power for us to tap into. Merely tuning into what we physically feel in our bodies will tell us a great deal about our fears.

Scan your body section-by-section—start in your toes, then move to your arches, to your ankles, up your legs, into your hips, into your core, and so on. Note which parts feel light or heavy, sticky or free. Which parts feel tension? Be particularly mindful to identify where in your body you feel fear—or any emotion for that matter. Do you get butterflies in your stomach? Is your mind buzzing with energy? Or perhaps you hold it all in your shoulders. This scan is a great way to identify how you physically react to fear. Fear in the present situation will often show up as butterflies in our gut or tension in our shoulders. Our hip joints will often hold emotions that are pushed down and are not being voiced. These are just a few examples, and everyone is different.

Learn to do this scan regularly and in different situations. You'll begin to identify how your body responds to fear and other emotions, to what feels normal and what is new. Simply being curious and aware, without judgment, can help you move into, through, and beyond fear with a kind sense of self-love.

For many years, public speaking lit up my own pachad fear. I made up all kinds of unreasonable stories in my head—*I'll forget what I'm going to say, I'll trip, I won't inspire*—and I'd feel the nerves racing through my body. Then one day when I was at an event getting ready to speak at a session, an energetic healer woman I knew asked me if I'd like an energetic gift. I, of course, said yes, and she instinctively directed her hands to my core—my womb space. I could feel my body take in her strong gift of powerful energy as it surged into my soul. I stood in awe of the intense flow that filled my body from my core center, soaking in her warm, caring intention. I walked into that talk with a new foundation—on a different footing. I delivered that talk with confidence and ease and ultimately ended up bringing half the audience into my business as new clients.

What I soon discovered was that I have the power within to generate this flow simply by tuning into my body. I am able to transform the fearful gut energy into power energy. Today I know that, as a woman, my womb space is a power center. I don't require the wonderful energetic gift I was presented on that day—I have learned to feed my own core.

I know that my womb center is where I first feel fear in my body, when it comes to public speaking. And it may be that I will always experience fear shaking my body a bit in public speaking situations. I now know that's okay, because I understand that I can transform this energy into a power center by embracing the racing I feel and then treating it with love and tenderness. I can close my eyes and envision a bright shining light radiating from my core. I can imagine this light finding and helping those who will benefit from my own gifts.

Take time to get to know your body's wisdom. She can be your guide through fear. There is a fine dance between letting that energy stop you and letting that energy lift you up. Test the boundary and step out on the edge.

Mind Games

Our mind can play all kinds of tricks on us when it comes to fear. We merely need to stop and look beneath the surface of the crazy tennis match flow of thoughts that invade our thinking when fear steps in.

A few of my favorite ways to work with fear that manifest into mind games are straight from Mohr's fear toolkit.

Follow fear through to the end game. Particularly in pachad, our mind is often drumming up big stories of unlikely possibilities. For example, in my own public speaking fear, I might have imagined falling off the stage. I merely need to ask, "And then what?" When I start to think this through to what might actually happen, I see that I'd probably pull myself up with a rush of people running up to me to make sure I'm okay. I'd be embarrassed. "And then what?" I'd probably make light of it and joke about it. "And then what?" I might start off my talk feeling a little rattled. "And then what?" I'd deliver my talk. This line of thinking can be carried out until you arrive at the realization that there's absolutely nothing life threatening that is likely to happen.

Our pachad fears are based on our human instinct of fight or flight when we lived in life-or-death situations. We rarely face life-or-death situations in our present-day lives. In fact, most often when pachad shows up, it's showing up as an emotional fear, not a physical fear. Realize that we often paint scenarios in our minds of things that might occur, but they're not really likely to happen. There is great power in looking into the eyes of fear when we walk through the "and then what?" scenarios.

Another one of Mohr's great tactics to address fear is to shift into curiosity. As she states, "It's very hard for curiosity and fear to exist simultaneously."

When Elizabeth Gilbert was on Oprah's "The Life You Want" tour, she shared on her Facebook page, "I was sitting between Iyanla Vanzant and Deepak Chopra, and one seat away from Rob Bell, which was making me dizzy and amazed. I had more than one moment of, 'What in the world am I doing here with these great beings?' Also, I was looking around that stadium realizing, 'Tomorrow morning, I have to speak to these thousands of people.'"

Later, Gilbert shared that she found her courage when she took the stage simply by being curious about who was in the audience. She put on a "helping" mindset—a "how might I help the people who are here" frame of mind, which took her mind off herself. This brilliant shift of curiosity let her shine her light and her gifts in an even bigger presence than she'd already created for herself.

I have learned to use Gilbert's trick in my own speaking. Today when I walk on a stage, I tune into the gifts that each person in the room has, knowing that they are meant to matter somehow to our great world and that I am about to light the spark of curiosity and possibility. This puts me into my own purpose role. Instead of it being about me and my performance, it's about them and what can unfold—it's about creating the ripple effect.

You can apply curiosity to any nerve-rattling circumstance. Consider what you might learn from the others at a meeting that feels intimidating. Consider how you might help even one person in a roomful of people. Consider how you might grow simply by stepping into that fear, and consider what new possibilities might unfold because of your courage.

Heartfelt Compassion for Your Fear

One of the most important lessons about moving through fear is to apply gentle love to your fear. As Mohr claims, "Fear also can't exist in the presence of love." That day I stood with Windy Day, I invited love into the round pen. I acknowledged that fear is a normal part of every journey. If you stop to get to know her with an open heart filled with compassion, she will recognize that you've acknowledged her and she will also begin to open her firm grasp and set you free.

Today when I take a stage, I still feel the flittering wings of a hummingbird dancing in my core—and I do choose with intent the hummingbird analogy rather than the butterfly. For me, hummingbirds represent joy and fill me with a sense of wonder and fascination. They are playful and dart about with focused intention. It's that very energy combined with love—love for myself, love for the people sitting in the room, love for the work that has called me—that sets my fear free. As my fear takes wings and leaves, I'm uplifted with light and a new set of empowerment wings that uplift me into my own strength. That is transformation. Transformation gifted through love.

Elizabeth Gilbert said, "In actuality, fear doesn't even deserve this lofty treatment. It's not a defining characteristic for anyone. Here's what I'm going to tell you about your fear: It's the most boring thing about you. The most interesting thing about you is your creativity, your passion, your love, your joy, your faith—all that stuff is fascinating."

My final note on fear is: "Don't let your fears define you!" See them, know them, experience them. Most importantly, learn to move through them and take the risks that are calling to you. Step out on the edge of your comfort zone and dance in all that you stand for in this world.

Another obstacle that can slow and even stop our journey to our purpose is scarcity thinking. Do you worry about not having enough money, clients, wisdom, expertise, or courage? Scarcity breeds more scarcity. Learning to approach your journey with an abundance mindset will shift the pace of your spiraling journey faster than any other factor. Let's look at ways that scarcity thinking might show up in your life and address how you can move into abundance.

The energetic flow of scarcity can come in many ways. Let's start with money, because that's one of the most common drivers during times of change. When I was starting my business, money was of course not flowing at the same levels as it had in my corporate days. A perfect storm for scarcity thinking.

However, I inherently knew that I needed to breathe positive energy into abundance.

One book I particularly enjoyed at this time was the *Dynamic Laws of Prosperity* by Catherine Ponder. Ponder had an exercise that I used diligently with each new paying client. As I went through the bank drive-thru window and passed my deposit through the tube, I stopped in my own private ceremony and stated, "I give thanks that this $100 is but a symbol of the inexhaustible substance of the Universe. I give thanks that ten times this amount (or $1,000) is now coming to me and quickly manifests for me in perfect ways."

I had this saying written on a post-it note that I kept in the console of my car for the first several years in my business. As I sent my deposit off to the bank teller, I'd sit in my car and say these words out loud. And do you know what happened? My business continued to grow exponentially each year. I learned that there is great power in setting positive intention with focus and consistency.

Author Lynne Twist, in her book, *The Soul of Money*, wrote, "What you appreciate appreciates." She encourages people to envision the flow of finances to us and then to others, investing in causes for which we care. By shifting our thinking into flowing energy that will come to us in abundance and flow to others in abundance, we set free the clutching grasp of scarcity mindset.

I invite you to practice the power of abundant financial

thinking that masters such as Ponder and Twist have shared. Practice it and notice what begins to happen.

Another form of scarcity thinking I see a lot is in the form of competition. People wrap their arms around their "competitive space." They speak poorly about their competition. They don't collaborate with someone who might be competition. Mind you, the irony is not lost on this former marketing exec where competitive analysis was king. But wisdom has given me a new-found understanding and appreciation of competition.

What I believe today is that if you have done your work about who you are and what you stand for, you're moving from a unique space that no one else in the world can own. If you're working from your essence, taking courageous steps into your gifts and how you're meant to matter, no one can or will own the same marketing space you own. There are people who need your specific gifts, and there are people who need your competitors' gifts. Your job is to understand what makes you unique and special and how to find those who need your unique and special gifts. Your job is to weave the Essence of You—perhaps not the specific words you chose in your Essence Statement, but the qualities that exist within—into your personal or corporate brand. This is what will set you apart from the others and open doors to collaboration.

Embrace others working in your field with love and appreciation for their unique gifts. I promise there will be more combustible power that comes forth from an abundant state of mind in partnership and collaboration than from the scarcity mindset. Don't fall into the energetic stream of scarcity, focusing energy on what's wrong with others and why you're better.

Instead, shine your gifts out in proud abundance, embrace others in your field of work for their unique expressions, and let the energy of good flow.

> *"... There are no wrong turns, only unexpected paths."*
> ~ Mark Nepo

Your spiraling journey through change is ever-evolving and constantly flowing. The beautiful thing is that you get to decide on the pace by being aware of the messages from your body, mind, and heart, and through learning to dance in the moment. I invite you to relax into your goals and enjoy the ride of discovery, knowing that it won't be a straight line and acknowledging that every turn you make will bring you new wisdom.

A final note to leave you with is my recommendation that you get help and put support systems around you. My teachers, mentors, and coaches—in both the "people form" and the "animal and nature form"—have helped me assimilate what I know today. I would have never made the changes, taken the risks, celebrated my stumbles, and tried again, had it not been for the wonderful guides that encouraged me to keep going, play bigger, expand, grow, and evolve. I'm forever thankful for their wisdom and their belief in me.

In an interview in her podcast radio series, Glambition Radio, Ali Brown said, "The reason most people don't survive being entrepreneurs, business owners, or even climbing the corporate ladder is not that they fail. It's that they can't take the heat. They give up."

Learn to embrace the heat. Don't give up. Embody your firedancer spirit. This is your journey and you have gifts to give to the world. There are people waiting today for YOU!

Reflection

1. Consider what fears you might have. List them. Give them a voice—stating them out loud. Then play the "what if" game. What if that happens, so what? Keep working through the possibilities. Set your fears free.
2. A great way to move through fear is to move! Go out in nature on a walk and move your body. Extend your hands into the air and feel the freedom and power this movement can create.
3. Consider who some of your competitors are in your work. Reach out to one of them with a collaborative intent. See what unfolds!

Power of Perseverance

Breakthrough to the other side takes perseverance. A galloping rhythm of muscle, sweat and determination, grounded by a steady focus on your destination.

If you feel your path begin to sway, anchor back to your course, keeping sight on that place where your heart is drawn. Engage your inner engines and feel the power that builds within.

The more you feed this power, the more the momentum gains. Feed the power through connections. Right people, right action and positive thinking. Open your mind to the possibilities and let colors add new dimensions, unthought of before. Feel the momentum take you into a full-on gallop.

For this is your ride. You only need set in place the actions and plans to manifest it. Engage your power within!

15

Lighting the Fire of Your Calling

"... the people who are crazy enough to
change the world are the ones who do."
~Steve Jobs

It's time to own your gifts and acknowledge how you matter. Knowing who you are at your essence and how you're meant to matter is important. Stepping into all your light and owning your gifts is even more vital. Not stepping into the shining power of you would be like owning a Ferrari and keeping it hidden in the darkness of your garage, never experiencing its full power, speed, and smooth agility.

It's time to start embodying your essence and purpose. When I say embody, I do mean that it's time for you to step into your power from head to foot, to energetically feel this in your core—your power center. For a moment, I want you to stand and place your hands a few inches below your belly button. Feel this space that pulses beneath your hands—the place in your body that fills the space between your hand and your spine. This is your power center. Breathe into this space and consider your essence. Breathe into how you're meant to matter. This is where we're going to start.

In Amy Cuddy's TedTalk, "Your Body Language Shapes Who You Are," Cuddy shares how the simple movement of raising your arms up high into the air expands your energetic space bigger and out into the world. She says, "Fake it 'til you make it." Keep practicing putting yourself out there. This is a potent addition to connecting into your power center. Try it on for size. Feel it. Fake it 'til you make it.

In my Equine Vision Journey retreats, I often have participants walk around the arena and send out big intentions for how they want to matter—starting at their power center and then raising their arms high as they make powerful declaration statements. It's with big voices, big intentions, and big movement that they start to feel the power of their inner-Ferrari rise to the surface. That's the energy level you're looking for when you embody your gifts and purpose.

How Do You Resonate?

I want you to consider for a moment different people in your life and how they make you feel. Some people, by just being in their presence, will energize you and create a kind of "buzz of enthusiasm" for life and living, which you begin to feel yourself. Others will deplete your energy. You'll leave their presence feeling worn out and exhausted. The energy that these two types of people resonate is very different. There are all kinds of energies in between. When we open up our bodies to the experience of different energies, we can feel them. This is how people resonate.

It matters what energy you put out into the world. It's true that you will resonate different energies and frequencies at different times in your life, depending on what is going on in your world at the time. When you're on fire with excitement, you will vibrate differently than when you've lost someone close to you in your life. Yet, I always believe that there is a conscious choice we can make about how we show up in the world— even in the most difficult situations. I believe that we're exactly where we are supposed to be in our life at any given moment. I believe there is a silver lining in every experience we move through on our spiraling journey—and even in the most difficult situations we can ground ourselves in the bigger purpose of our lives. I believe we create our worlds through the language we use, the way we embody our journey, and how we manage our day-to-day lives.

So consider for a moment how you resonate to others. When

you're embodying your purpose and doing things you love, I can promise you that your shining light will resonate brighter and uplift others around you. This is how you create a legacy that matters.

When you step into your Essence of You, life changes. The scattered, too-many-things-to-do rhythm of life transforms into intentional sparks of empowerment in a stream of positive flowing life energy. Things come easily and windows open wide. The heart settles into a place of deep contentment. Obstacles melt away to shine light on possibilities that were always there.

Developing Your Brand

This journey to the understanding of who you are, how you matter, and how you shine your light into the world is the foundation of your personal brand. Your personal brand is how people experience you—how you show up in life, how you dress, how you represent what you stand for in both your work and personal life. At the end of the day, it's how you make people feel.

What this doesn't mean is that you have a work-you and a personal-life-you. I hear this so often from women I meet: "I'm a different person at work than I am in my personal life." The **brand of you**—no matter who you are—is grounded in your authentic self. It's not different at work than it is at home. It's just you. I invite you to master the art of translating this newfound awareness of who you are into how people consistently experience you.

Another key part of defining your personal brand requires understanding to whom you want to matter—your tribe—and knowing how you want to help them and what you want to be known for, whether it's in your work environment, volunteer opportunities, or your personal life.

People make our world go round. It's highly likely you cannot step into a life that matters without a tribe of people around you. Chances are you're going to have to step out and expand your circle of influence and network of connections.

And I'm talking about real connections, not the kind of stick-your-business-card-into-the-face-of-as-many-people-as-you-can "connecting," but meaningful connections of shared support. This means you need to get to know the people in your tribe—those people in whose lives you want to make a difference. It means understanding what they need in their lives and approaching every connection with, "How I can I help you?" If you approach these new connections with a helping energy, the reciprocal will flow back exponentially.

In my last working years of the corporate world, I worked so many hours that I made no time for connections. The day I left that job I had six connections on LinkedIn. My network was limited to the people with whom I worked every day. I wasn't set up for transition. It took a lot of time and diligence to change this, but today, I have a network in my life of amazing women doing amazing things. Some are clients, some are influencers, some are dear friends—all of them are based in real relationship.

A couple of tips for making meaningful, long-lasting connections with your tribe:

1. Always approach the people in your tribe with "How can I help you?"
2. Get to know what makes your tribe tick—what excites them, what is keeping them awake at night, what emotions dance in their lives?
3. Get to know where your tribe hangs out. Get engaged.
4. Consider if there is a way to connect with your tribe in shared meaning. I sit on a couple of different nonprofit boards, surrounding myself with my tribe. We get the opportunity to work together on causes that make a difference. This is a beautiful way to connect.
5. Skip the speed networking environments that are all about meeting as many people as you can.
6. Connect with people around your passions. If you like to hike, join a mountain club. If you like to run, meet other runners. If you like to read, join a book club. There's something for everyone.
7. Nurture the connections you do make. Reach out to people occasionally to see what's going on in their life. Go to coffee or out for a glass of wine. Make it personal and real.

At the end of the day, it's about expanding who you know, showing up authentically in your full essence every day, and when asked, being clear about what it is you stand for. This is how consistent personal brands are built—by being you, by resonating positive energy, and by growing your connections.

Reflection

1. Who is your tribe—those to whom you want to matter? Where do you find them?
2. What do you want to be known for in your work? In your personal life? In your volunteer work?
3. How do you want people to experience you?
4. How might you represent your brand in the words you choose to represent you? What feelings do you want to invoke?
5. How might you represent your brand in colors? How might you represent your brand in the clothing you wear?

Fire Horses

Deep inside there is an inner strength. A fire power. Fire power breathes life into our souls when we need it most. It is there for the taking – we only need call upon it.

The essence of power radiates from the horse. It has come into your life today to lift you, to carry you to the top of the mountain with ease, elevating you to new heights and offering beams of untapped wisdom.

As you reach the summit of this mountain, fire power moves through your body, intuitively seeking a healing path within where healing strength is most craved. Let fire power do its work today. Feel its strength. See its light. Embody its spirit of elevation. Anything is possible, for you are filled with the strength of Fire Horses.

16

Golden Spiral

*"The most beautiful thing we can experience is the
mysterious. It is the source of all true art and science."*
~ Albert Einstein

In your journey through this book, I have referenced the spiral effect of our lives many times. When we understand our gifts and step into them, adding positive energy and effort, we spiral upward into new possibilities. As we explore, learn, and grow, feeding our journey with new wisdom, our lives are uplifted and expanded. It is here that the synchronicity of life flows to us easily—our spiral expands upward quickly, effortlessly, and abundantly.

Conversely, when we dwell in negativity and resistance, we

fall prey to our spiral of life slowing down, and even spiraling into a downward direction. It's a choice you get to make. Taking time to discover your purpose in life—your reason for being here—will provide a roadmap toward happiness and fulfilment.

Over the years of working with clients, I have often found myself drawing spiraling pathways in the air with my index finger, highlighting the evolving growth and expansion in their lives. I have used this visual in moments when I am helping them see that they're exactly on the path they're meant to be on—that they are collecting life experiences that are broadening each cycle, evolving and building a foundation that is aligned with why they are here on this earth. They often nod their head in excitement as they begin to connect the dots and see the possibilities that can unfold in the journey before them.

When I look back through years of my personal journals, I realize that I've been drawing spirals most of my life. When I would sit idly on a conference call, I often subconsciously doodled a spiral. I didn't know where this natural inclination—this gut instinct—to tune into this pattern came from. But it's apparently been trying to catch my attention my whole life.

One day, as I was about halfway through writing this book, a cousin in New York posted a link on Facebook that referenced the golden spiral. The Facebook post had a beautiful picture of spiraling energy that caught my eye. When I clicked through to the link, I saw photo after photo of this energy as it exists in nature—in the flow of our galaxy, in the center of a sunflower, in the arching spiral of a succulent plant, in the base of a pinecone, in the curve of a ram's horns, in the cochlear shape of our inner ear, to the tail of a seahorse (of which I have a tattoo, by the way), to the twist of a seashell. All these images brought me back to the seashell I found at 16,000 feet. It seemed that life was coming full circle.

I reached out to my cousin with excitement, "What is this about? Tell me more!"

And so she pointed me on my own spiraling journey of discovery. This is what I learned. "In geometry, a golden spiral is a logarithmic spiral whose growth factor is π [symbol for pi], the golden ratio. That is, a golden spiral gets wider (or further from its origin) by a factor of π [symbol for pi] for every quarter turn it makes." [from Wikipedia]

Consider for a moment the spiral of a seashell. Each spiral from its center becomes broader and wider, expanding for the growth of its inhabitant. And while all the mathematicians of the world might get excited about the pattern of numbers that are replicated in the Fibonacci formulas—the sequence of numbers that creates these geometrical curvatures—I was interested in the energetic knowing that lived within me.

This was exactly the phenomena I had been working in with my clients and in my own life. As our wisdom grew, as the experiences of our lives broadened into new realms, our spiraling shells of life expanded and opened up to the world. It was this phenomenon that I had tuned into in the past as I doodled spiral drawings in my notes. I was fascinated.

What was this energetic flow that pulled me in? Did I know this energy flow at a soul level? Do we live the journey of our lives in the same natural phenomenon that exists in our Universe amongst the seashells and the galaxies—a giant spiraling effect of growth? Could it be that the evolution of flow that brings growth and new ideas and new people and new paths into our world is fueled by this same energetic flow?

I believe it is—and I believe it is this same energy that leads us to our purpose, if only we open our hearts and hear the messages that are there to hear. For this is a life well lived.

It's a tragedy for anyone to live in a numbed state when there is so much more to experience through our connections with ourselves, with others, and with all the Universe. We are one, and what we bring into the world matters. We can choose to participate in our earth's evolution or we can choose to denigrate it—to add to the chaos.

When we choose to live into our fullest potential, we find the natural spiral of our own lives. The spiral of our life starts from knowing our inner self—our essence—and connecting to the wisdom and signposts that nature and the Universe provide. Living through the natural spiral of our lives allows us to feel, to learn, to experience. We step into a realm of inner knowing we didn't even know existed. That inner knowing guides us in our choices. We realize our work of exploration and growth is never done, but rather it's always changing and evolving. It's our journey.

Our journey is not a roadmap—there's not a final destination. You are an evolving, ever-growing soul. And when you claim your role in this great world—the role meant specifically for you—then you have found your seashell. Then you have begun your journey where your own spiraling growth will move and evolve in each cycle of discovery, expansion, and action—taking you into your journey and your purpose. Remember, you have gifts to give to this world. Who are you to withhold them?

Reflection

1. Go to my website KamiGuildner.com/Firedancer and view my slideshow of Spirals in Nature.

2. Go into nature and find your own examples of the golden spiral. They are everywhere. If you are able, bring an example home and add it to your nature shrine. Or take a photo and put it just inside your journal for a constant reminder that life is always evolving, growing, and expanding.

3. Your Spiraling Life Journey: Take out a large sheet of paper and a set of colorful pens. Draw a line horizontally across the center. On the bottom half of the sheet of paper, begin to draw the spirals in your life that have brought you to this point in your life—identifying the key milestones that have occurred. For example, you might have a spiral that is about college, another about getting married and having children, and yet another about that big job you first took, etc. The circles can be of varying sizes and the spiral can move upward or sideways. It's your life journey that you're mapping. As you near the horizontal line, know that you are beginning to cross into the future spirals of your life. Continue your spiral drawing onto the top half of the sheet, labeling the future milestones of your dreams.

Circles of Life

We move through the circles in our lives each hour, each day, each season, each year. With each new cycle, we add more experiences and leave old experiences behind. The beautiful patterns that weave their presence into your being become the very essence of you. These gifts are ever-evolving – never still.

Stop and feel the flow of this energy as it moves through your body today. These wheels of life move at different speeds and change in size and color. They represent relationships, personal growth, family, career and community. Consider which cycles are most alive in your world. Which resonate most strongly in this moment? How do these circles of life influence the patterns you live?

The ever-moving nature of these circles tells you that there is always change afoot. Embrace this nature. Play in the lessons that live within the glowing, colorful movement. There is something to be learned. Breathe into the flow and let it feed your soul – your heart. Grow.

Closing

I am awestruck at the lessons that have come forth from that small spiraling seashell I found at the top of that cold Tibetan mountaintop. The significance of that seashell was unbeknownst to me on that day. At the time, I only realized the great geological journey that shell had taken. Little did I know the symbolic wisdom and universal forces at work to place that seashell in my path on that particular day.

Our soul journeys in ways that are unforeseeable, yet if we stop to connect the dots of our life stories that rise to the surface, we can see a mystical pattern of purpose—the great hand of the Universe at work. This is what I have learned from this shell—my spiral shell that has magically shaped my own journey.

I wrote the story about finding that seashell long before I started this book. When I started to write this book, something reminded me to pull this writing out from the archives … and intuitively I knew that it belonged up front. I didn't know why and certainly hadn't connected the dots.

This is the beauty of our soul journey. There is a grand purpose in our intuitive knowing, our experiences, the people we meet, and even the choices we make. In each and every curve that we take in this spiraling evolution in life, the Universe provides opportunities for us to find and discover why we're here on this earth. We only have to be aware—to learn to listen to and hear our inner wisdom and to make space to let it blossom.

My hope for you is that this soul journey has awakened new awareness and trust. You journeyed into this lifetime with gifts that matter. And now more than ever, the world needs you to step into your purpose with connected clarity.

I invite you to ignite the journey before you with intention. Share your gifts with your tribe that needs you. Live large. Expand your thinking beyond your wildest dreams. Play in the what-ifs and push your Self beyond your edges of comfort. Live as firedancer.

My final gift to you is my favorite card from my *Pony Ponderings Inspiration Cards*, "Dancing on the Edge." May these words bring inspiration to your journey.

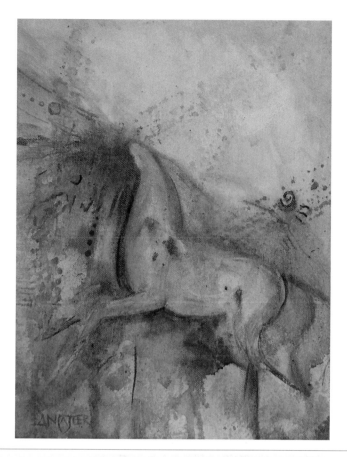

Dancing on the Edge

Shine the spotlight onto the world before you. Dance on the edge and feel your inner strength as you step beyond a world of comfort. Break through to new realms – unknown realms – and let the power of uncertainty unfold.

For today is a day to break through the boundaries – real or imagined. Today is a day to dance in the new possibilities that unfold when you expand your horizons. Leaping with faith into this unknown, knowing that the landing might be a bit bumpy, but more importantly, knowing that you will find your footing and each step will become stronger.

For this is about taking risk – a risk that will feed your body with invigoration, engaging the very being of your nerve endings. Feel the electricity of this energy and embrace it. Feed it with the grounding of the earth, and know that it will move you into a bigger world with more possibilities. Take a chance on this day. Push the boundaries before you further. Live fully into your world as it expands."

Pledge to live large in your life and dance on the edge. Grow and explore and invite your heart to voice all that it can be. Step into your soul's purpose and share it with the world.

The Essence of You

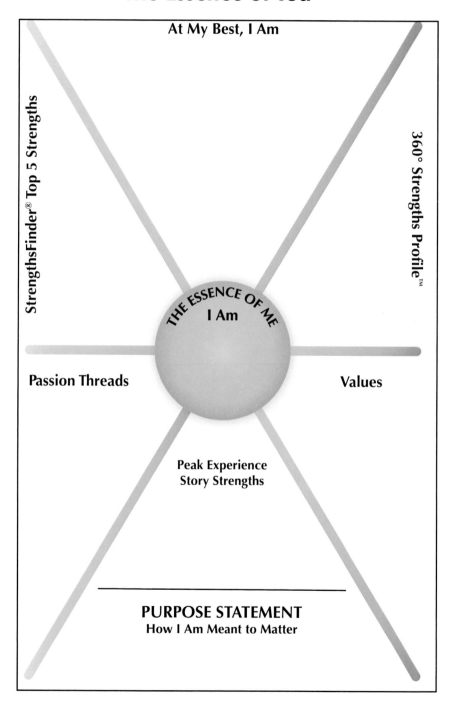

At My Best, I Am

StrengthsFinder® Top 5 Strengths

360° Strengths Profile™

THE ESSENCE OF ME
I Am

Passion Threads

Values

Peak Experience
Story Strengths

PURPOSE STATEMENT
How I Am Meant to Matter

Your Journey Continues ...

"Imagine all the people living life in peace.
You may say I'm a dreamer, but I'm not the only one.
I hope someday you'll join us, and the world will be as one."
~ John Lennon

Imagine for a moment a world where people live fully out loud, into their brightest light—they are on fire with passion, purpose, and meaning. Can you feel the energetic shift that would occur? Imagine if each person used their light to make a difference in the lives of others. Can you see the ripple effect this would create?

This vision starts with you. You are a catalyst to this vision. You were born with a unique set of gifts that are meant to matter. Are you willing to commit to owning who you are and the gifts you were given to serve in this lifetime? Are you willing to step into your full light, even in the moments that scare you out of your wits and throw turmoil into your balancing act of grace? When you commit to living into your reason for being on this earth, something shifts. You discover a strength of courage you didn't know existed within you. You experience a gift of flowing abundance that somehow works out in ways you never expected. You grow and find that you have more gifts hidden just beneath the surface.

I'd like you to reflect back on the lessons you've learned from *Firedancer*. Consider which five lessons could best serve your own spiraling journey that lies before you and will define your future—that will shape your impact. I invite you take a moment to write these lessons down. Even better, paint them into a beautiful picture or image so that you can display them in a prominent place and see them often.

My hope for you is that your spiral of life takes you to new unknowns filled with beauty, passion, and love. Continue to feed your spiral journey with intentional inspiration and nature-gifted introspection. Make space to hear those whispers in your heart that will guide your choices with inner wisdom and awareness.

I'll leave you with a few final questions to ponder ... Where do you want to be in one year? What if nothing has changed? How would that feel? You've opened the door to new possibilities simply by playing in the questions ... your questions ... and listening to your inner wisdom. This is the chance to redefine the legacy you will leave—to share your story in a grander way.

Before you ever picked up this book, I believed in your story. I believe you can do it. This is the story of your life. You can make a huge difference in our world. You only need to commit to living into your soul journey each and every day.

Usually it doesn't take long for my clients to start to see and share the amazing transformations that occur in their lives. They're surprised, grateful, and energetically shifted as the spiral in their lives accelerates and evolves into an ever-changing spiral of new possibilities. This can happen to you, too. You just have to stay actively engaged with your journey and put into practice what you've learned here.

I invite you to keep me posted about your life journey. Share with me what has shifted in your world—the new opportunities that have come your way, the doors that have opened that were invisible before, the courageous moments when you stepped out just beyond the edge of what was comfortable, the ways in which you've made a difference.

Beyond this book, I am here to support you. If you would like assistance with any part of your journey, I am available to you. There are several ways for you to access me. The first is my website, KamiGuildner.com. There, you will find a lot of free resources, including blog posts and videos. On my website, you can also learn about my various programs, which include:

▲ Extraordinary Women On Fire Group Program, where you can join other extraordinary souls in shared support and inspiration.

▲ Private one-on-one coaching with me or any of my strategic partners.

▲ Extraordinary Women Connect – a series of intimate events for wildly successful women to connect in meaning, purpose, and shared support.

▲ My Equine Vision Journey Retreats and other nature-inspired events.

If you enjoyed the Pony Ponderings card postings at the end of each chapter, the entire deck of *Pony Ponderings Inspiration Cards* is available for purchase on my website. This full deck contains fifty beautifully-illustrated daily inspiration cards to bring positive, thought-provoking guidance to your soul path. Inspired by the heart and wisdom of horses, the messages provide a pathway to your deepest inner knowledge, playfully engaging your mind, body, emotions, and spirit. If you would like to receive a complimentary thirty-day daily Pony Ponderings inspiration via email, sign up at KamiGuildner.com/Firedancer. If Diana Lancaster's artwork inspires you as it does me, I invite you to visit her website at http://dianalancaster.com/.

You can also join my Kami Guildner Coaching Facebook community at Facebook.com/KamiGuildnerCoaching, where I regularly share inspiration and create community.

Additionally, I am available for speaking engagements and to visit your book club. If your book club reads *Firedancer*, I would be honored to come and speak to your book club in person or visit virtually via Skype.

Whether we meet in person someday or not, my hope is that through *Firedancer*, we have joined in the common pool of connection. A ripple effect that will generate from me to you. A ripple effect that will move from you to others. Together, we make a difference upon the world and create a shift. Can you feel it? Can you see its beauty? Shine your light out into the world—for YOU are meant to matter!

Acknowledgments

From the early visions of writing a book to today, as I sit making final edits, I never could have imagined the twists and turns of lessons that would come my way throughout this process. I am extremely grateful for the many wise souls who came into my world at just the right moment to help me birth and shape this book into reality.

Thank you, Donna Mazzitelli, my brilliant editor who helped me get unstuck when I didn't know how. Thank you for your kind inner wisdom that knew when to push me to go deeper and even invited me to expand my own understanding of this big amazing ride we're on. Thank you for your encouragement, your guiding vision, and for holding my hand through every evolution that unfolded in creating *Firedancer*.

I'd also like to extend a special thank you to Diana Lancaster, my partner in *Pony Ponderings Inspiration Cards*.

Together we created this deck of fifty cards—with her artwork and my writing—which you have sampled at the end of each chapter in this book. From the moment I saw her artwork, I knew it was perfect for the deck of cards I had envisioned. The words flowed effortlessly from me when I wrote Pony Ponderings because of the beauty of her work.

Thank you to my wonderful friend and strategic partner, Sarah Bohnenkamp, for reading my book from cover to cover and for providing insights and suggestions to make this book even better. You inspire me every day, and I am so fortunate to get to collaborate, work, and play with such a brilliant bright soul.

A huge thank you to the wonderful clients who have shared their journeys with me. I learn every day from the extraordinary souls who have graced my pathway. I'm inspired by your courage, your bright lights, and the impact that you are making in our world. Without you, this book never would have been possible.

There are so many mentors and teachers who have helped me find me, evolve my calling, and define the work I do today.

Thank you, Ariana Strozzi of Skyhorse Ranch, who taught me the wonders of Equine Guided Coaching. You guided me back into the ancient wisdom of horses and nature that my soul longed for. You are a pioneer in this magical, mystical work and have opened the world for me and so many others who are making a difference in the world. The moment I discovered your work, I knew and trusted it—and this gave me the courage to follow this dream—to say yes to this calling in my life.

Thank you, Amanda Trosten Bloom, for helping me rediscover my own gifts in your teachings and for introducing me to the whole field of Appreciative Inquiry that has shaped my own coaching programs from the very beginning.

Thank you to Tommi Wolfe, Rachael Jayne Groover, and Datta Groover for teaching me to step up and play bigger in my work—to step into my fears, to find and trust my voice, and to put my work out in the world. Thank you for encouraging me in uplifting support when my knees shook and my voice faltered, and for helping me to stay committed, to learn, and to grow.

I would be remiss if I did not thank the Syzygy herd of horses that graces my backyard and guides my retreats. They have brought wisdom and inner whispers to my own journey— providing awareness, new visions, and opening within. May I always be in awe of the gifts you bring. Here is to you: Destiny Dancer, Dakota Jack, Zip Zap Cadillac, and Brown Sugar Special (Sugaree). You make my world brighter.

Thank you to my wonderful family who has shaped my world. While I have spoken often of my father throughout this book, my mother holds equal hero status. Thank you, Mom, for your strength, your belief in me, and your love. You are such an important role model in my life—you taught me positivity, perseverance, and love for life. Thank you for patiently listening to me read parts of my book over the phone and for always being my biggest cheerleader in life. Your unwavering belief in me has been a foundation of strength for me throughout my whole life.

I also put out a big thank you to my sister, who is one of my dearest friends and confidants. And to my brother, who always makes me laugh and loves all of our family big and deeply.

Thank you, of course, to my beautiful soulful son, Josh, who

I love bigger than life itself. Your love of life and big loving heart lights up my world every day. You are such an important part of my whole grand journey. I cherish our deep connection as mom and son. These threads of connection are interwoven into every page of this book.

I finish my gratitude list with the biggest thank you to the love of my life, my knight in shining armor, my husband, Tim. Tim, you have been such a gift in my life. Your love makes me stronger every day. You held me up when times were tough. It was you who encouraged me to step onto this new journey of life. You believed in me when I doubted my abilities. Your daily encouragement, throughout the early visions of this book to the final signoffs, has helped me believe in me. Your love and strength and easy way of being have made my world safe and happy. Thank you for the beautiful love story we have built together.

About the Author

Kami Guildner is a woods-walker. A sky-gazer. A horse-lover. Raised on the wide open plains of Colorado, against the majestic Rocky Mountains, wilderness fueled her soul from an early age. With a young enchanted mind, she gained an early understanding that the natural world brings clarity, provides space to dream, and opens our eyes to views of worlds unseen before us.

Her early dreams journeyed her into a wildly successful twenty-year executive career. Yet, deep in her heart, she was hearing a calling for something more. Whispers. An inner knowing. Her reconnection to this inner knowing provided by nature opened up her own world of transition—from executive to entrepreneur.

Today, Kami helps executives, entrepreneurs, and truth-seekers around the world "Live Out Loud" into a passionate and meaningful life. Leading them to connect to their inner gifts, discover new meaning and new paths, her clients step into intentional action fueled with vitality and courage. In addition, Kami founded Extraordinary Women Connect™—a series of intimate events for wildly successful women to connect in meaning, purpose, and shared support.

Kami brings her many years of leadership, marketing, strategic planning, and business growth expertise to her clients. She holds a BS from the University of Colorado at Denver in International Business and Marketing and is trained in Appreciative Inquiry change management methodology, holding a certificate in the Practice of Positive Change. Kami is also a SkyHorse EGE™ Certified Equine Guided Coach. To learn more about Kami and her work, go to KamiGuildner.com.

More Praise for
Firedancer...

Sometimes the best insights come from those who've suffered great loss, like Kami Guildner, whose super-charged life came to an abrupt halt when her lucrative marketing job was phased out and, a month later, her beloved father passed away. In *Firedancer: Your Spiral Journey to a Life of Passion and Purpose,* Guildner skillfully integrates her own story from Colorado farm girl to corporate go-getter to women's life coach with advice on how to find and follow your true calling.

Guildner's book—a cross between business-style mentoring and New Age inspiration—delivers an "anything is possible" message in a straightforward style that appeals to both professionals and more esoteric truth-seekers. And the client examples, from the woman who rediscovered her artistic side and used it to help veterans to another who quit her high-tech position to launch her own company, are crafted with depth and compassion. Each chapter ends with a "Reflection" questionnaire and a "Pony Ponderings Inspiration Card"—an abstract equine illustration and message that may be a little off-putting to those uncomfortable with the metaphysical approach.

Nevertheless, *Firedancer* accomplishes a great deal. It encourages. It helps peel away excuses. And it motivates us to embrace our dreams, no matter how far-fetched. Chapter 14, "Emotions, Roadblocks and Obstacles," addresses a particularly important issue: fear—of competition, of failure, of not making enough money. "By shifting our thinking into flowing energy that will come to us in abundance and flow to others in abundance,"

Guildner writes, "we set free the clutching grasp of scarcity mindset."

Readers open to New Age thought, and who simply want to re-claim childhood pastimes that once made them feel happy and whole, will enjoy *Firedancer*. And those who feel empty and lost will find comfort in Guildner's words: "Your gift is meant to matter, and ... there are people who need your gift. Who are you to withhold this gift from the world?"

—Blue Ink Review

About the Press

Merry Dissonance Press is a book producer/indie publisher of works of transformation, inspiration, exploration, and illumination. MDP takes a holistic approach to bringing books into the world that make a little noise and create dissonance within the whole in order that ALL can be resolved to produce beautiful harmonies.

Merry Dissonance Press works with its authors every step of the way to craft the finest books and help promote them. Dedicated to publishing award-winning books, we strive to support talented writers and assist them to discover, claim, and refine their own distinct voice. **Merry Dissonance Press** is the place where collaboration and facilitation of our shared human experiences join together to make a difference in our world.

Visit http://merrydissonancepress.com/ for more information.